LABORATORY MANUAL
TO ACCOMPANY

AN INVITATION TO SPANISH

THIRD EDITION

LABORATORY MANUAL
TO ACCOMPANY

PUNTOS DE PARTIDA

AN INVITATION TO SPANISH
THIRD EDITION

MARÍA SABLÓ-YATES

McGraw-Hill Publishing Company

New York St. Louis San Francisco Auckland Bogotá Caracas
Hamburg Lisbon London Madrid Mexico Milan
Montreal New Delhi Oklahoma City Paris San Juan
São Paulo Singapore Sydney Tokyo Toronto

This is an ⊟ book

Lab Manual to accompany
Puntos de partida, Third Edition

2 3 4 5 6 7 8 9 0 MAL MAL 8 9 4 3 2 1 0 9

ISBN: 0-07-557400-4

Project editor: Marie Deer
Typesetter: Margaret Hines
Art editor: Lorna Lo
Cover designer: Juan Vargas, Vargas/Williams Design
Illustrators: Stan Tusan, Barbara Reinertson, Katherine Tillotson, Axelle Fortier
Printer and binder: Malloy Lithographing, Inc.

Grateful acknowledgment is made for use of the following materials: *page 20* Instituto Superior de Intérpretes y Traductores; *21* Escuela Superior de Estudios de Marketing; *30 Diario de Juarez*, Editora del Norte; *49* © Antonio Mingote; *84* © Quino; *103 top left* Casa Glez; *top right* Chopin; *bottom left* Microstar; *bottom right* Audio Bonpland; *112* Amoblamiento 2000; *137 top* Instituto Roit; *bottom* Laboratorio Sais; *140* © Quino; *147* Hotel Argentino; *153* © Antonio Mingote; *178* Megacentro; *181* © Antonio Mingote; *185 Semana; 186 Semana; 188* Grupo Banco Exterior; *191* © Quino; *195 top* © Ediciones Sedmay; *195 bottom* Ali. Reprinted with permission; *214* Riviera Paquetes; *221* Universidad de Cantabria; *223* © Quino

Contents

To the Student

In the tape program to accompany the third edition of *Puntos de partida,* you will find a variety of exercises to help you become more proficient in the use of the Spanish language. The third edition of the tape program has been substantially rewritten to reflect the text's increased emphasis on contextualized practice, functional language usage, and cultural content, and to incorporate more types of listening comprehension exercises and activities, including exercises based on realia and exercises in which you will interact with the speakers on the tape. We hope that the changes in format and content will provide a natural context within which you will begin to communicate in Spanish!

The tape program follows the format of chapters in the text. Each chapter begins with a section (*Vocabulario: Preparación*) in which vocabulary is practiced in a variety of contexts. This preliminary vocabulary study is followed by pronunciation exercises (*Pronunciación y ortografía*), the minidialogues from the text, followed by exercises and activities on the grammatical concepts of the chapters (*Minidiálogos y gramática*), and functional dialogue practice (*Situaciones*). Each chapter ends with a section (*Un poco de todo*) in which all grammar points and vocabulary introduced in the chapter are combined. You will find additional review sections (*Repasos*) after chapters 3, 6, 9, 12, 15, and 18. An effort has been made to reintroduce vocabulary and grammar from previous chapters in these review sections and throughout the Laboratory Manual, so that you have the opportunity to use the grammatical structures and vocabulary you have learned in a variety of contexts and situations. Exercises and activities in most sequences progress from controlled to more open-ended and personalized or interactive, to give you a chance to be creative in Spanish while practicing the skills you have learned.

Although the tape program includes some material taken directly from *Puntos de partida,* it also contains much that will be totally new to you: contextualized exercises (including question-and-answer sequences and interviews), dictations, personalized questions, visually based listening comprehension exercises, cultural listening passages (you will find these in the *Un poco de todo* and *Repaso* sections), activities based on realia, additional brief dialogues, some interactive in nature, and—beginning in *Capítulo 11*—songs.

The following types of exercises are a regular feature of the *Puntos de partida* tape program and can be found in most chapters.

• *Definiciones, Situaciones,* and *Asociaciones* use a multiple choice or matching format in order to test listening comprehension and vocabulary. *Identificaciones* and *Descripción,* as their names imply, will ask you to generate responses based on visuals, with or without written or oral cues. Although these are more controlled in nature, they are all contextualized and related to the theme of the current or a previous chapter.

• In addition to the *Minidiálogos* from the text, the manual includes thematic dialogues not taken from the text (*Diálogos*). They are offered for listening comprehension, and you will answer questions or true/false items based on them. They offer examples of real-life situations and often convey cultural information.

• *Conversación* is the title for the functional minidialogues taken from the text and any other conversation in which you are asked to take the role of one of the speakers after you have listened to the model conversation. At times you will be asked to use cues that are given in your manual; on other occasions you can let your own experience guide you in your answers. The *Conversación* dialogues will give you a chance to engage in everyday types of conversations.

• There are two types of question-and-answer sequences, *Preguntas* and *Entrevista. Preguntas* are more controlled in that an oral or written cue is given. The correct answer is heard on the tape after each item. The *Entrevistas*, on the other hand, are more open-ended and personalized. They give you practice in answering as well as asking questions. They usually appear at the end of a grammar section or in the *Un poco de todo* or *Repaso* sections, and they recombine vocabulary and grammar from the current chapter or previous chapters. Although possible answers are given for some of the *Entrevista* exercises, many do not offer responses. Your instructor may want you to tape your answers so that he or she can listen to them later.

• The Laboratory Manual also includes many types of dictations (*Dictados*). You will be asked to listen for and write down specific letters, words, phrases, or entire sentences. One variation of the dictation format involves listening to a conversation or series of brief conversations and writing down a list of requested information. Your ability to listen for specific information in Spanish will be enhanced by these types of exercises.

In the Laboratory Manual itself, you will find the exercises for the pronunciation sections, model sentences for most vocabulary and grammar exercises, visuals on which activities are based, the text of most of the *Conversación* dialogues, and the words to the songs. The text for the minidialogues, the listening passages, and other listening comprehension exercises is not provided in the Laboratory Manual, since these are offered for listening comprehension practice.

Answers to any exercise called *Dictado* are provided in the back of the manual. Answers to most other exercises are given on the tape immediately after the item, and time is allowed for you to repeat the correct answer. Answers to listening comprehension exercises and activities are given after each item or at the end of the series of items, so that you know immediately whether you understood the exercise. Answers to the exercises based on the Listening Passage in the *Un poco de todo* sections are given at the end of the tape, after a ten-second pause.

Visuals are used to illustrate and provide a context for the minidialogues. There are also a number of visually based activities. Time is provided on the tape for you to scan the drawings, but you may wish to stop the tape to take more time to "look" if you need it. A number of cartoons are also included, with conversational activities based on them. In addition, the third edition contains a number of pieces of realia (real things, such as advertisements, classified ads, and so on, that you would encounter if you were in a

Spanish-speaking country). Here again, time for scanning is provided on the tape; take more time if you need it.

Sound effects are used throughout the tape program, when appropriate. You will hear a variety of native speakers, so that you can get used to the variety of accents and voice types found in the Spanish-speaking world, but no accent will be so pronounced as to be difficult for you to understand. In most parts of the tape program, speakers will speak at a natural or close to natural speed (particularly in exercises for which the text is provided in the manual).

We offer our sincere thanks to the following individuals: to Marc Accornero, whose voice is heard on the songs and who was instrumental in their selection; to Thalia Dorwick, without whose help, support, and superior editing this Laboratory Manual and tape program would not have been possible; and to Ron Yates and Jean and Duquesne Sabló for their constant support throughout the writing process.

Ante todo

PRIMERA PARTE

SALUDOS Y EXPRESIONES DE CORTESÍA

A. *Diálogos.* In the following dialogues, you will practice greeting others appropriately in Spanish. The dialogues will be read with pauses for repetition. After each dialogue, you will hear a summarizing statement. Circle the number of the statement that best describes each dialogue. First, listen.

1. ANA: Hola, José.

   JOSÉ: ¿Qué tal, Ana?

   ANA: Así así. ¿Y tú?

   JOSÉ: ¡Muy bien! Hasta mañana, ¿eh?

   ANA: Adiós.

Comprensión: a (b)

2. SEÑOR ALONSO: Buenas tardes, señorita López.

   SEÑORITA LÓPEZ: Muy buenas, señor Alonso. ¿Cómo está?

   SEÑOR ALONSO: Bien, gracias. ¿Y usted?

   SEÑORITA LÓPEZ: Muy bien, gracias. Adiós.

   SEÑOR ALONSO: Hasta luego.

Comprensión: a (b)

3. MARÍA: Buenos días, profesora.

   PROFESORA: Buenos días. ¿Cómo se llama usted?

   MARÍA: Me llamo María Sánchez.

   PROFESORA: Mucho gusto.

   MARÍA: Encantada.

Comprensión: (a) b

B. *Otros saludos y expresiones de cortesía.* Repeat the following sentences, imitating the speaker.

1. ¿Cómo estás, Alberto?

2. ¿Cómo te llamas?

3. Encantada, señorita.

4. Muchas gracias, Juan.

5. De nada, Elena.

6. Con permiso, señora.

7. ¡Perdón!

8. Por favor, Ana.

9. Buenas noches, Julio.

C. *¿Qué dicen estas personas?* (What are these people saying?) Circle the letter of the drawing that is best described by the sentences you hear. Each will be said twice.

1. a)   b)

2. a)   b)

3. a)   b)

4. a)   b)

CH. *Situaciones.* You will hear a series of questions or statements. Give an appropriate response for each. The answer you hear is not the only possible answer, but repeat it anyway after you hear it!

1. ...   2. ...   3. ...   4. ...   5. ...   6. ...

PRONUNCIACIÓN Y ORTOGRAFÍA: EL ALFABETO ESPAÑOL

A. You will hear the names of the letters in the Spanish alphabet, along with a list of place names. Listen and repeat, imitating the speaker. Notice that most Spanish consonants are pronounced differently than in English. In future chapters, you will have a chance to practice the pronunciation of most of these letters individually.

a	a	la Argentina	n	ene	Nicaragua
b	be	Bolivia	ñ	eñe	España
c	ce	Cáceres	o	o	Oviedo
ch	che	Chile	p	pe	Panamá
d	de	Durango	qu	cu	Quito
e	e	el Ecuador	r	ere	el Perú
f	efe	la Florida	rr	erre	Monterrey
g	ge	Guatemala	s	ese	San Juan
h	hache	Honduras	t	te	Toledo
i	i	Ibiza	u	u	El Uruguay
j	jota	Jalisco	v	ve	Venezuela
k	ca	(Kansas)	w	doble ve	(Washington)
l	ele	Lima	x	equis	Extremadura
ll	elle	Sevilla	y	i griega	Paraguay
m	eme	México	z	zeta	Zaragoza

B. Repeat the following words, imitating the speaker and paying close attention to the difference in pronunciation between Spanish and English.

1. j   José   junio   Jamaica   Julio

2. h   hotel   Héctor   La Habana   historia

3. ñ   la Coruña   cabaña   señor   niña

4. ll, y   Castilla   cordillera   Yolanda

5. g   agua   Guillermo   Germán   gitano

6. c   Caracas   Colón   vicuña   Cecilia

C. You will hear a series of words. Each will be said twice. Circle the Spanish consonant used to spell each word.

1. l (ll)
2. (n) ñ
3. h (j)
4. (b) g
5. j (g)
6. c (ch)

CH. *Dictado*: ¿Cómo se escriben estos nombres?* (How are these names written?) You will hear the spelling of a series of Hispanic proper names. Write out each name and pronounce it.

MODELO: (te-o-eme-a acentuada-ese) → <u>Tomás</u>

1. <u>Héctor</u>
2. <u>eñrica</u>
3. <u>Yolanda</u>
4. <u>peguna</u>
5. <u>Conche</u>
6. <u>Juana</u>

LOS COGNADOS

A. Repeat the following cognates, imitating the speaker.

1. cruel
2. idealista
3. paciente
4. generosa
5. tímido
6. introvertido
7. terrible
8. religioso
9. emocional
10. seria

B. *¿Quiere aprender un idioma extranjero?* (Do you want to learn a foreign language?) Listen to the following ad for foreign-language classes given by *Idiomas Serrano*. It is from a Spanish newspaper. Then try to find the Spanish equivalent of the following English words. (Remember to repeat the answer.)

1. teaching staff   Profesorad
2. native   nativo
3. visit us   Visitentos
4. environment   Ambiente
5. methodology   Metodologia

INGLES - FRANCES
ALEMAN - ESPAÑOL

IDIOMAS SERRANO

Profesorado nativo. Metodología moderna. Técnica audiovisual. Ambiente agradable. Profesionalidad y eficacia ¡VISITENOS!

SERRANO 68
TELEFS. 275 39 60 93

---

*Answers to all *Dictado* exercises are given in the Appendix.

C. *Dictado: ¿Cómo son?* (What are they like?) You will hear five sentences. Each will be said twice. Listen carefully and write the missing words.

1. Nicolás es *pessimesta*.

2. La profesora Díaz es *intelgente*.

3. Don Juan no es *serio*.

4. Maite es muy *eficiente*.

5. Íñigo no es *sentimental*.

¿CÓMO ES USTED?

A. *Descripción.* Describe these people, using the oral cues. (Remember to repeat the correct answer.)

MODELO: (él / optimista) → <u>Él es optimista.</u>

1. ...   2. ...   3. ...   4. ...

B. *¿Cómo es usted?* What kind of person are you? Describe yourself, using the oral cues. Remember that if you are female, the final *-o* must be changed to *-a*. The answer you will hear is not the only possible answer.

MODELO: (generoso) → <u>Soy generosa.</u> or <u>No soy generosa.</u>

1. ...   2. ...   3. ...   4. ...   5. ...

C. *Entrevista.* Ask the following persons about their personalities, using *¿Eres...?* or *¿Es usted... ?*, as appropriate, and the cues you will hear. Follow the model. (Remember to repeat the correct answer.)

MODELO: Marta (tímida) › <u>Marta, ¿eres tímida?</u>

1. Ramón...   3. Señor Moreno...

2. Señora Alba...   4. Anita...

SEGUNDA PARTE

MÁS COGNADOS

A. *Descripción.* In this exercise, you will practice gisting, that is, getting the main idea, an important skill in language learning. Although some of the vocabulary you hear will not be familiar to you, concentrate on the words that you *do* know. After the exercise, you will be asked to choose a statement that best describes the passage.

1 ②

B. *Dictado: Asociaciones.* For each of the following categories, you will hear a series of three words. Each series will be said twice. Write only the word or words you associate with each category. In this exercise, you will practice listening for specific information.

1. Naciones: _italia_

2. Instrumentos musicales: _piano clanete_

3. Personas: _Roanca tourista_

4. Animales: _tigere_

5. Cosas (*Things*): _radio libro_

C. *¿Qué es esto?* (What is this?) You will hear a series of cognates. Each will be said twice. Repeat each one, telling in what category it belongs. First, listen to the list of categories.

un lugar (*a place*)	una bebida (*a drink*)
un deporte (*a sport*)	un animal
un instrumento musical	un concepto

MODELO: (¿Qué es un rancho?) → <u>Es un lugar.</u>

1. ...   2. ...   3. ...   4. ...   5. ...   6. ...

PRONUNCIACIÓN Y ORTOGRAFÍA: LAS VOCALES: A, E, I, O, U

A. Repeat the following pairs of Spanish and English words, imitating the speaker. Note that Spanish vowels are short and tense; they are never drawn out with a *u* or *i* glide as in English.

say / se   *tee* / ti   *low* / lo   *to* / tú

B. Repeat the following Spanish syllables, imitating the speaker. Try to pronounce each vowel with a short, tense sound.

1. ma   fa   la   ta   pa

2. me   fe   le   te   pe

3. mi   fi   li   ti   pi

4. mo   fo   lo   to   po

5. mu   fu   lu   tu   pu

C. Repeat the following words, imitating the speaker. Be careful to avoid the English schwa, the "uh" sound. Remember to pronounce each vowel with a short and tense sound.

1. hasta   tal   nada   mañana   natural

2. me   qué   Pérez   usted   rebelde

3. así   señorita   permiso   imposible   tímido

4. yo   con   cómo   noches   profesor

5. uno   tú   mucho   Perú   Lupe

CH. *Dictado.* Listen carefully to the following words. Each will be said twice. Write the missing vowels.

1. p_a_s_o_
2. c_a_s_a_
3. m_e_s_a_

4. c_i_n_e_
5. p_e_s_a_r
6. m_i_s_a_

LOS NÚMEROS 0-30

A. *Las bolsas* (money exchanges) *internacionales.* You will hear a series of numbers from the following chart. Each will be said twice. Circle the number you hear and repeat each number. The word *coma* means comma; it is used instead of the decimal point in many Hispanic countries. In this exercise, you will practice listening for specific information.

Indicadores de Bolsas Internacionales	
País	
USA	7,2
Japón	14,4
Alemania	5,6
Francia	6,2
R. Unido	8,0
Holanda	4,3
Suiza	7,0
Suecia	7,8
Italia	6,3
España	4,1

B. *¿Cuánto es?* (How much does it cost?) You will hear the price of three different brands of items you want to purchase. Repeat the price of the most expensive brand. In this exercise, you will practice listening for specific information. (Remember to repeat the correct answer.)

1. ...   2. ...   3. ...   4. ...

C. *Dictado.* You will hear eight numbers. Each will be said twice. Write out the number you hear in the corresponding place.

6 _seis_
13 _trece_
24 _vientecuatro_
2 _Dos_

0 _serio_
3 _tres_
28 _viente ocho_
12 _Doce_

CH. *¿Qué hay en la sala de clase?* (What is there in the classroom?) You will hear a series of questions. Each will be said twice. Answer based on the following drawing.

1. ...   2. ...   3. ...   4. ...

GUSTOS Y PREFERENCIAS

A. *Preguntas.* Ask a friend whether he or she likes the items mentioned in the cues you will hear.

MODELO: (la universidad) → ¿Te gusta la universidad?

1. ...   2. ...   3. ...   4. ...   5. ...

B. *¿Qué te gusta?* (What do you like?) Listen to the following conversation about preferences.

—¿Te gusta el béisbol?
—Sí, me gusta, pero (*but*) me gusta más (*more*) el vólibol.

Now you will hear a series of questions. Each will be said twice. Answer them, following the model of the conversation you have just heard and using the written cues. (Remember to repeat the correct answer.)

1. Sí,... / tocar (*to play*) el violín

2. Sí,... / la música popular

3. Sí,... / el tenis

4. Sí,... / beber (*to drink*) café

C. *Entrevista.* You will hear four questions about your likes and dislikes. Each will be said twice. Answer based on your own preferences. You will hear a possible answer on the tape. (Remember to repeat the answer.)

1. ...   2. ...   3. ...   4. ...

TERCERA PARTE

¿QUÉ HORA ES?

A. *¿Qué hora es?* Answer according to the drawings after you hear the corresponding number.

1.

2.

3.

4.

5.

6.

B. *¿A qué hora es... ?* Your friend wants to know at what time the events you will hear take place. Answer, using the written cues. You will hear a possible answer on the tape. (Remember to repeat the answer.)

MODELO: (¿A qué hora es la excursión?) 10:00 A.M. → A las diez de la mañana.

1. 8:45 P.M.

2. 1:50 P.M.

3. 4:40 P.M.

4. 12:53 P.M.

5. 11:35 A.M.

C. *Entrevista.* You will hear a series of questions. Each will be said twice. Answer based on your own experience. You will hear a possible answer on the tape. First, listen to some words that may help you answer some of the questions.

comer (*to eat*)   mirar (*to watch*)   jugar (*to play a game*)

1. ...   2. ...   3. ...   4. ...   5. ...   6. ...

LAS PALABRAS INTERROGATIVAS: UN RESUMEN

A. *Preguntas* (Questions). Your friend Antonio has just made some statements that you didn't quite understand. You will hear each statement twice. Indicate the interrogative word or phrase you should use to obtain information about what he said.

1. (a) ¿cuándo?   b) ¿cuánto?

2. (a) ¿cómo es?   (b) ¿dónde?

3. (a) ¿cuántos?   (b) ¿dónde?

4. (a) ¿cuántos?   b) ¿a qué hora?

5. (a) ¿qué es?   b) ¿cómo está?

6. a) ¿cuál?   (b) ¿a qué hora?

B. *Dictado*. You will hear six questions. Each will be said twice. Write each question next to the appropriate drawing.

1. _____Donde esta_____

2. _____Ov cuanto es e chcolata_____

3. _____quienes estaiante_____

4. _____Que esto_____

5. _____a que hor excursion_____

6. _____aue es capital_____

MANDATOS Y FRASES COMUNES EN LA CLASE

A. Repeat the following sentences, imitating the speaker.

Otra vez, por favor.   No sé la respuesta.

No entiendo.   Sí, cómo no.

Tengo una pregunta.   Espere un momento, por favor.

B. *¿Qué acaba de decir el profesor?* (What did the professor just say?) The following drawings show a classroom in which a professor has just given several commands. You will hear each of his commands twice. Write the number of each command next to the corresponding drawing.

a. 2/3    b. 1/2

c. <u>3</u>
<u>4</u>

ch. <u>4</u>
<u>1</u>

C. *Situaciones*. In this exercise, you will practice using the classroom expressions listed below. You will hear four situations. Choose an appropriate reaction to each and say it. First, listen to the list of expressions. ¡OJO! Not all the expressions will be used. (Remember to repeat the correct answer.)

No sé la respuesta.
Otra vez, por favor. No entiendo.
Sí, cómo no.

¿Cómo se dice _____ en español?
Tengo una pregunta.

1. ...   2. ...   3. ...   4. ...

REPASO

A. *En el periódico* (newspaper). You will hear a series of headlines from a Spanish newspaper. Each will be said twice. Write the number of each headline next to the section of the newspaper in which it most likely appears. Try not to be distracted by unfamiliar vocabulary; concentrate instead on the main idea of the headline. First, listen to the sections.

<u>3</u> Política

<u>4</u> Libros (*Books*)

<u>1</u> Espectáculos (*Entertainment*)

<u>5</u> Deportes (*Sports*)

<u>2</u> Economía

B. *Listening Passage*. You will hear a brief passage about where Spanish is spoken. It will be read twice. Then you will hear a series of statements about the passage. Circle *C* if the statement is true (*cierto*) or *F* if it is false (*falso*). (Answers to this exercise are given at the end of the tape.)
    You will hear a few new words as well as some cognates in the passage. Try to guess the meaning of these words from context.

1. ~~C~~ (F)   2. C (F)   3. (C) F

C. *Y para terminar... Conversaciones*. You will hear two conversations that are partially printed in your manual. When each conversation is read for the second time, play the role of Alberto and complete it with appropriate expressions. You will hear a possible answer on the tape.

1. Alberto y la señora Cruz, 3:00 P.M.

    ALBERTO: Buenas <u>días</u>.

    SRA. CRUZ: Muy buenas, Alberto. ¿Cómo estás?

ALBERTO: <u>May</u>. ¿<u>bien</u>?

SRA. CRUZ: Muy bien, gracias. Hasta luego, Alberto.

ALBERTO: <u>Hasta luego</u>

2. Alberto y Susana, estudiantes, 9:00 A.M.

SUSANA: Buenos días. ¿Cómo te llamas?

ALBERTO: <u>Me</u>. <u>llamo</u>. ¿<u>Alberto</u>?

SUSANA: Me llamo Susana.

ALBERTO: <u>Mucho gusta</u>

SUSANA: Encantada, Alberto.

Capítulo 1

PRIMERA PARTE

VOCABULARIO: PREPARACIÓN

A. *Asociaciones*. A friend is describing a series of locations. Try to guess the locations he is describing. Write the number of the description next to the location. In this exercise, you will practice getting the general idea in spite of unfamiliar vocabulary. First, listen to the list of locations.

____4____ un cuarto (*room*) en la residencia ____3____ una biblioteca

____1____ una oficina ____2____ una sala de clase

B. *Identificaciones*. You will hear a series of sentences that describe the items in the drawing. Give the number that corresponds to each identification, then repeat the sentence. First, look at the drawing. (Remember to repeat the correct answer.)

1. ... 2. ... 3. ... 4. ... 5. ... 6. ... 7. ... 8. ... 9. ... 10. ...

C. *¿Es hombre o mujer* (man or woman)? You will hear a series of nouns that refer to people. Identify each by telling whether the person is male or female. In this exercise, you will practice listening for specific information—here, the definite article and the noun ending to determine gender. (Remember to repeat the correct answer.)

MODELO: (¿La profesora?) → <u>Es mujer.</u>

1. ... 2. ... 3. ... 4. ... 5. ...

CH. *En la biblioteca*. You work at the reserve desk at the library and you are organizing the books for this semester. Which books correspond to which classes? You will hear the names of the books twice. Circle the letter of the most appropriate choice.

1. (a) Es para una clase de matemáticas.   b) Es para una clase de sicología.

2. a) Es para una clase de comercio. b) Es para una clase de inglés.

3. a) Es para una clase de español. b) Es para una clase de ciencias naturales.

4. a) Es para una clase de computación. b) Es para una clase de historia.

D. *¿Qué estudian?* You will hear a brief paragraph about what Raquel and Fernando study. It will be said twice. Listen carefully and circle the names of the subjects that each person studies. In this exercise, you will practice listening for specific information. The word *facultad* means school or division, as in Law School or Humanities Division.

Raquel estudia... física anatomía computación sicología biología

Fernando estudia... español ciencias políticas comercio biología inglés geografía historia

E. *Conversación: En el* campus. You will hear a conversation, partially printed in your manual, in which a woman asks for the location of the History Department on campus. Then you will participate in a similar conversation about another department. Complete it by telling where that department is on your own campus. You will hear a possible answer on the tape.

—Por favor, ¿dónde está el departamento de historia?

—Está en el edificio Graduate studies.

—Muchas gracias.

—_____

PRONUNCIACIÓN Y ORTOGRAFÍA: *DIPHTHONGS AND LINKING*

A. Repeat the following words, paying close attention to the pronunciation of the indicated vowels.

Weak vowels:

(i) Pili jirafa practicar presidente

(u) gusto lugar Cuba universidad

Strong vowels:

(a) Ana nada patata calabaza

(e) trece elefante clase general

(o) los dólar novela político

B. Diphthongs are formed by two successive weak vowels (*i* or *y, u*) or by a combination of a weak vowel and a strong vowel (*a, e, o*). The two vowels are pronounced as a single syllable. Repeat the following words containing diphthongs.

1. (ia) historia gracias

2. (ie) bien siete

3. (io) Julio adiós

4. (iu) ciudad (*city*) viuda (*widow*)

5. (oi) soy estoy

6. (ua) Eduardo Managua

7. (ue) buenos nueve

8. (uo) cuota arduo

9. (au) auto aumentar

10. (eu) Ceuta deuda (*debt*)

11. (ai) aire hay

12. (ui) ¡cuidado! (*careful!*) fui (*I was/went*)

13. (ei) veinte treinta

C. Diphthongs can occur within a word or between words, causing the words to be "linked" and pronounced as one long word. Repeat the following phrases, imitating the speaker.

1. (oi/ia) Armando y Alicia

2. (ci/ic) el tigre y el chimpancé

3. (ai/iu) Elena y Humberto

CH. Linking also occurs naturally between many word boundaries in Spanish. Repeat the following sentences and phrases, saying each without pause as if it were one long word.

1. ¿Dónde está la capital?   4. Puerto Rico y el Canadá

2. tu auto y tu estéreo   5. Colorado y Nuevo México

3. Tomás y Pilar   6. un jugador de fútbol

D. *Dictado.* You will hear four sentences. Each will be said twice. Listen carefully and write what you hear.

1. _Alicia es no_____

2. _Dalia es estudia Espanol_____

3. _Como esta Usted_____

4. _A veinteisiete estudiar, én clase hoy_____

MINIDIÁLOGOS Y GRAMÁTICA

1. Identifying People and Things: Singular Nouns: Gender and Articles

A. *Minidiálogo: En la clase: El primer día.* You will hear a dialogue followed by a series of statements about the dialogue. Circle *C* if the statement is true (*cierto*) or *F* if it is false (*falso*). In this exercise, you will practice listening for specific information.

1. C (F)   2. C (F)   3. (C) F

B. *¿Qué te gusta?* Tell a friend what you like, using the oral cues and the correct definite article. (Remember to repeat the correct answer.)

MODELO: (librería) → Me gusta <u>la librería</u>.

1. ...   2. ...   3. ...   4. ...   5. ...

C. *¿Qué hay en el cuarto* (room)? Identify the items in the room after you hear the corresponding number. Begin each sentence with *Hay un...* or *Hay una...* (Remember to repeat the correct answer.)

CH. *Dictado: ¿Quién? ¿Dónde? ¿Qué?* You will hear a series of words. Each will be said twice. Repeat each word and write it in the appropriate category.

Personas	Edificios o lugares	Cosas
dependiente		Residencia
mujer	boligrifo	Hotel
secretario	mesa	universidad

2. Identifying People and Things: Nouns and Articles: Plural Forms

A. *Dictado: Escenas de la universidad: Una oficina desordenada* (messy). You will hear a brief description of Professor Adán's office. It will be read twice. Write the names of the objects in his office, in the appropriate column, singular or plural. The articles are given for you.

Singular

el _____*profesor*_____

un _____*boligrfo*_____

un _____

Plural

unos _____*papel*_____

unos _____*libros*_____

las _____

unos _____

B. You will hear a series of phrases. Give the plural form of the first four nouns and articles and the singular form of the next four. (Remember to repeat the correct answer.)

Singular → plural

1. ...   2. ...   3. ...   4. ...

Plural → singular

5. ...   6. ...   7. ...   8. ...

C. *Identificaciones.* You will hear a series of words. Each will be said twice. Circle the letter of the person or persons to whom the words might refer.

1. (a)) María y Teresa   b) la señorita Rojas

2. a) Luisa y Ana   (b)) Tomás y Carolina

3. a) Alberto   (b)) Ángela

4. a) los profesores   (b)) las mujeres

CH. *Los errores de Pablo.* You will hear some statements that your friend Pablo makes about the following drawing. He is wrong and you must correct him. (Remember to repeat the correct answer.)

MODELO: (Hay dos libros.) → <u>No. Hay tres libros.</u>

1. ...   2. ...   3. ...   4. ...   5. ...   6. ...

SEGUNDA PARTE

3. Expressing Actions: Subject Pronouns: Present Tense of -ar verbs: Negation

A. *Minidiálogo: Una fiesta para los estudiantes extranjeros.* You will hear a dialogue followed by a series of statements about the dialogue. Circle *C* if the statement is true (*cierto*) or *F* if it is false (*falso*). In this exercise, you will practice listening for specific information.

1. C Ⓕ   2. Ⓒ F   3. Ⓒ F̶

B. *Hablando de estudios.* The following ads for courses appeared in various Hispanic newspapers. Glance at them and decide which course or courses each of the people described on the tape should take. First, skim the ads, focusing on cognates and key phrases. (You have ten seconds to look at the ads. Begin now.)

a. (3)

El **Instituto Superior de Intérpretes y Traductores**

Informa que están abiertas las inscripciones para las

LICENCIATURAS en TRADUCCION y en
INTERPRETACION.

LOS EXAMENES DE SELECCION seran los días
Agosto 19, 24 y 26

Interesados llamar a los teléfonos:
566-77-22 y 566-83-12 o acudir a:
RIO RHIN Nº 40, México 5, D.F.

ISIT

Acuerdos de validez oficial Nos. 3765 y 3655, Junio 20, 1980

UNA OPCION DE
ESTUDIO DIFERENTE

b. (1)

c. (2)

ch.

Mercedes: _____

Tina: _____

Pablo: _____

C. *¿Quién habla?* Answer the questions according to the model.

MODELO: (¿Quién? ¿Ud.?) → <u>Sí, yo</u>.

1. ...   2. ...   3. ...   4. ...   5. ...   6. ...

CH. *Dictado: Mi amiga y yo.* You will hear the speaker make a series of statements about herself and a friend. Each will be said twice. Listen carefully and write the verb forms you hear next to the correct subject pronoun. ¡OJO! Remember that subject pronouns are not always used in Spanish and that the verb ending will tell you who the subject is.

ella: _____

nosotras: _____, _____

yo: _____, _____

D. *Mis compañeros y yo.* Form complete sentences about yourself and others, using the oral and written cues. Do not repeat the subject pronouns unless they are needed. (Remember to repeat the correct answer.)

1. yo
2. nosotras
3. Luisa
4. el estudiante extranjero

5. profesora, Ud. ...
6. Jaime, tú...
7. Ana y Roberto
8. yo

E. *Entrevista.* You are a new student at this university, and some recent acquaintances are asking you about your life on campus. You will hear each question twice. Answer the questions according to your own experience. You will hear a possible answer on the tape.

1. ...   2. ...   3. ...   4. quiero...   5. prefiero...   6. ...

4. Getting Information: Asking Yes/No Questions

A. *Minidiálogo: En una universidad: La oficina de matrícula.* You will hear a dialogue followed by a series of statements. Circle the letter of the person who might have made each statement. In this exercise, you will practice listening for specific information.

1. (a)) la estudiante   b)) el consejero
2. (a)) la estudiante   b) el consejero
3. (a)) la estudiante   b) el consejero

B. *¿Es una pregunta?* You will hear a series of statements or questions. Listen carefully and circle the appropriate letter. Pay close attention to intonation.

1. a) statement   b)) question
2. (a)) statement   (b)) question
3. (a)) statement   b) question
4. a) statement   (b)) question
5. (a)) statement   (b)) question

C. *Entrevista con la profesora Villegas.* Interview Professor Villegas for your school newspaper, using the following cues. Use the *Ud.* form of the verbs. Use the subject pronoun *Ud.* in your first question only. Professor Villegas will answer your questions.

MODELO: (enseñar / inglés) → ¿Enseña Ud. inglés? (No, enseño español.)

1. enseñar / cuatro clases
2. enseñar / italiano
3. trabajar / por la noche

4. hablar / ruso
5. gustar / la universidad

SITUACIONES

En la biblioteca: Estudiando con un amigo

You will hear a brief conversation, partially printed in your manual, about studying. Then you will participate in a similar conversation. Complete it based on the cues suggested. You will hear the correct answer on the tape.

—Oye, ¿ _Quando es ~~estaranda~~ t Clase de computación_?

—A las _tres y media_. ¿Qué hora es?

— _Son las tres menos cuarto_ .

—Hay tiempo todavía. ¿No quieres estudiar diez minutos más?

—Está bien. Entonces, ¿qué tal si _pasamo por la librería_ antes de tu clase?

—¡De acuerdo!

Here are the cues for your conversation:

clase de computación
2:45
pasar por la librería

UN POCO DE TODO

A. *Definiciones*. You will hear a series of statements. Each will be said twice. Write the number of the statement next to the word that is best defined by that statement.

_3_ una profesora   _4_ un secretario

_6_ un cliente   _1_ el portugués

_2_ una biblioteca   _5_ los estudiantes

B. *Conversación: En la librería*. You will hear a conversation, partially printed in your manual, between two friends, David and Marcos. Then you will participate in a similar conversation. Complete it based on the sentences suggested.

DAVID: _____ .

MARCOS: Hola, David. ¿Qué tal?

DAVID: _____ .

MARCOS: Sí, trabajo aquí todos los días. Sólo tomo clases los lunes (*Mondays*) y los viernes (*Fridays*) por la mañana. ¿Qué necesitas?

DAVID: _____ .

MARCOS: ¡Y el dinero para pagar! Por eso (*That's why*) trabajo, David, por eso trabajo.

Listen to the sentences for your conversation. They are not in a logical sequence.

Bien, gracias. ¿Trabajas aquí en la librería?
Pues, necesito cuadernos, un lápiz y un diccionario. También necesito tres libros de texto.
Buenas tardes, Marcos.

C. *Listening Passage.* You will hear a brief passage about education in Hispanic countries. It will be read twice. Then you will hear a series of statements about the passage. Circle *C* if the statement is true (*cierto*) or *F* if it is false (*falso*). Answers to this exercise are given at the end of the tape.

1. C (F)   2. (C) F   3. C (F)   4. (C) F

CH. *Descripción.* Using the verbs you will hear, describe the actions in the drawing. You will hear a possible answer on the tape.

1. ...   2. ...   3. ...   4. ...   5. ...

D. *Y para terminar... Entrevista.* You will hear a series of questions. Each will be said twice. Answer based on your own experience. You will hear a possible answer on the tape.

1. ...   2. ...   3. ...   4. ...   5. ...

Capítulo 2

PRIMERA PARTE

VOCABULARIO: PREPARACIÓN

A. *La familia Muñoz.* You will hear a series of statements about the Muñoz family. Each will be said twice. Circle *C* if the statement is true (*cierto*) or *F* if it is false (*falso*). First, look at the family tree.

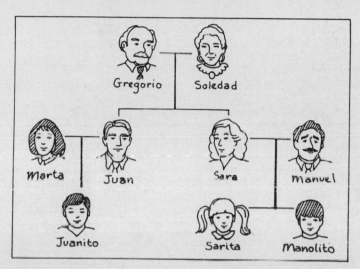

1. (C) F   2. (C) F   3. C (F)   4. (C) F   5. C (F)

B. *Conversación: Hablando de la familia.* You will hear a conversation, partially printed in your manual, about the number of people in a family. Then you will participate in a similar conversation. Complete it based on the cues suggested and using *tengo* to express "I have." You will hear the correct answer on the tape.

A: —Tienes una familia muy grande. ¿Cuántos son?

B: —Bueno, ~~tengo~~ cuatro hermanos una hermana .

A: —¿Y cuántos primos?

B: —¡Uf! ~~aaa tengo~~ un montón. Más de dieziseis .

Here are the cues for your conversation:

4 hermanos, 1 hermana
16

C. *¿Cuál es?* You will hear a series of descriptions. Each will be said twice. Circle the letter of the item or person described.

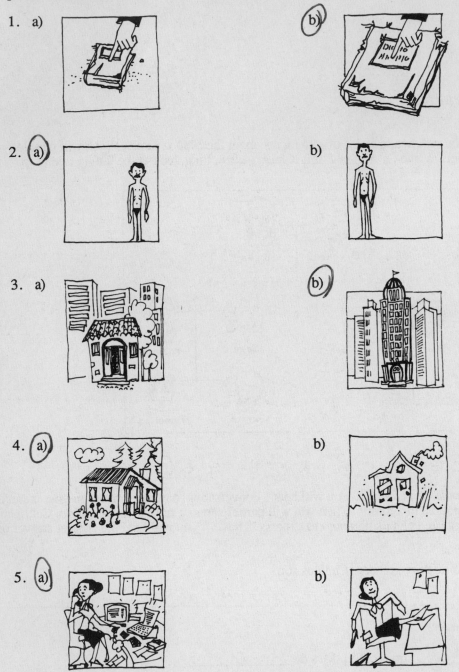

CH. *Descripciones: ¿Cómo son?* Describe the following fathers and their sons by using one adjective from each of the following pairs to answer the questions you will hear. You will hear a possible answer on the tape. First, listen to the adjectives.

alto / bajo

delgado / gordo

rubio / moreno

joven / viejo

MODELO: Miguel es _____, _____, _____ y _____.

1. ...   2. ...   3. ...   4. ...

D. *Dictado: El inventario.* You and a friend, Elisabet, are taking inventory at the university bookstore where you work. Write out the numerals as she dictates the list to you. She will say each number twice. ¡OJO! Items are given in random order. First, listen to the list of words.

___55___ mochilas   ___45___ novelas

_____ lápices   ___31___ calculadoras

___42___ cuadernos   _____ libros de texto

E. *En el periódico*. The following list of phone numbers is taken from a Hispanic newspaper. You will hear a series of questions about the numbers. Each will be said twice. Answer based on the list. First, look at the list. Don't be distracted by unfamiliar vocabulary.

MODELO: (¿Cuál es el teléfono de la Gerencia [*Manager*] General?) →
<u>Es el trece - cero nueve - cincuenta y cinco</u>.

EDITORA PASO DEL NORTE
FUNDADA EL DIA 17 DE FEBRERO DE 1976

OFICINAS Y TALLERES
Ave. Paseo Triunfo de la República y Anillo
Envolvente del Pronaf. Cd. Juárez, Chih. Mex.

PRESIDENTE Y DIRECTOR GENERAL
Osvaldo Rodríguez Borunda

JEFE DE REDACCION	*GERENTE DE PUBLICIDAD*
Jesús Luis Ceniceros Cervantes	Jorge Castro Obregón
JEFE DE INFORMACION	*DEPORTES*
Roberto Abrego Salazar	Ramón Guzmán Gallegos
SOCIALES	*RELACIONES PUBLICAS*
Esmeralda Torres B.	Jaime Martínez O.

TELEFONOS

Dirección General	13-08-16
Gerencia General	13-09-55
Jefatura de Redacción	13-28-64, 16-43-83
Jefatura de Información	13-28-64, 16-35-85
Información General	16-35-85, 13-28-64
Sociales y Deportes	13-82-87
Publicidad	13-02-44, 13-18-72
Clasificado	16-09-09, 16-03-76
Clasificado	16-09-66, 16-00-50
Administrador/Compras	16-16-85
Admón. Crédito y Cobranzas	13-28-86
Recepción/Suscripciones	16-00-06

REPRESENTANTES EN MEXICO
"LEMUS" Representaciones Periodísticas Tel. 286-02-02
OFICINAS EN CHIHUAHUA
Ave. Universidad No. 1502 Tel. 13-44-03, 13-45-85, 13-41-81
EN NUEVO CASAS GRANDES
5 de Mayo No. 400 y Alvaro Obregón Tel. 4-25-25
EL PASO, TEXAS.
10737 Gateway West Suite 108 Ph. (915) 595-07-32 595-07-42
SERVICIOS INFORMATIVOS
UPI, EXCELSIOR, REUTER y LEMUS
Precio del Ejemplar $400.00 Domingos $300.00

Atrasados el Doble

---

1. ...   2. ...   3. ...   4. ...

F. *Preguntas*. In this exercise, you will practice asking a friend information about herself and her family. Use the oral cues and any other necessary words. Repeat the question you hear. You will hear an answer to that question on the tape.

MODELO: (cómo / llamar) → ¿Cómo te llamas? (Me llamo Silvia.)

1. ...   2. ...   3. ...   4. ...

PRONUNCIACIÓN Y ORTOGRAFÍA: *STRESS AND WRITTEN ACCENT MARKS*

A. Repeat the following words, imitating the speaker. The italicized syllable receives the stress in pronunciation.

  • If a word ends in a vowel, *n*, or *s*, stress normally falls on the next-to-the-last syllable.

  *hi*jo   *al*to   sin*cer*a   intere*san*te

  • If a word ends in any other consonant, stress normally falls on the last syllable.

  trabaj*ar*   liber*al*   universi*dad*   profe*sor*

  • Any exception to these two rules will have a written accent mark on the stressed vowel.

  a*diós*   Ra*món*   fran*cés*   *Gó*mez   mate*má*ticas   sim*pá*tico

B. In words containing diphthongs, a written accent on the weak vowel will break the diphthong, causing it to be pronounced as two separate syllables. Two strong vowels together also result in two separate syllables. Repeat the following words, imitating the speaker.

1. dí-a   Marí-a

2. rí-o (*river*)   tí-o

3. con-ti-nú-e   gra-dú-e

4. a-e-ro-puer-to   a-or-ta   bo-a   re-or-ga-ni-zar

C. *Dictado.* You will hear the following words. Each will be said twice. Listen carefully and write in a written accent where required.

1. papa   4. nación   7. jóven

2. música   5. doctor   8. inteligénte

3. práctico   6. Marina   9. biológia

MINIDIÁLOGOS Y GRAMÁTICA

5. *Expressing* to be: *Present Tense of* ser; *Summary of Uses*

A. *Minidiálogo: En la oficina de la profesora Castro.* You will hear a dialogue followed by two statements about the dialogue. Circle the number of the statement that best summarizes the dialogue. In this exercise, you will practice listening for the main idea.

B. *¿Quiénes son?* Identify the following people, using the oral cues.

MODELO: José (mecánico) → <u>José es mecánico</u>.

1. Mariluz
2. el señor Barrios
3. tú
4. Tomás y Ernesto
5. Araceli y yo

C. *¿De dónde son?* Practice telling where people are from, using the oral cues.

MODELO: (María / México) → <u>María es de México</u>.

1. ...   2. ...   3. ...   4. ...   5. ...

CH. *¿Para quién son los regalos?* You need to give gifts to several of your relatives, and money is no object! Select appropriate gifts for them from the following list. First, listen to the list.

la calculadora
los libros de filosofía
los cien mil (*100,000*) dólares

la camioneta
las novelas románticas
los discos (*records*) de Madonna

Use the phrases *por eso, para ella,* and *para él,* as in the model.

MODELO: (Su [*Your*] hermano Juan es estudiante universitario.) →
<u>Por eso los libros de filosofía son para él</u>.

1. ...   2. ...   3. ...   4. ...   5. ...

D. *Entrevista: Opiniones.* You will hear a series of questions. Each will be said twice. Answer based on your own experience. You will hear a possible answer on the tape.

1. ...   2. ...   3. ...   4. ...

6. Describing: Adjectives: Gender, Number, and Position

A. *Descripciones.* You will hear four incomplete sentences followed by a series of adjectives. Each sentence will be said twice. Listen carefully and circle the adjective or adjectives that could be used to describe the person or persons mentioned in each sentence. Then repeat the completed sentence.

MODELO: (La señora Vásquez es...) → alto   rubia   simpática
<u>La señora Vázquez es rubia y simpática</u>.

1. (...) amables   inteligente   bonita
2. (...) paciente   bajos   gordo
3. (...) joven   romántica   optimista
4. (...) casados   perezosa   solteras

SEGUNDA PARTE

B. *Hablando* (Speaking) *de su familia: ¿Cómo son?* Practice telling what your family members are like, using the oral cues. Make any necessary changes in the adjectives you hear.

MODELO: (familia / rico) → <u>Mi familia es rica.</u>

1. ...   2. ...   3. ...   4. ...   5. ...

C. *¿De dónde son y qué idioma hablan?* Your friend Carmen is asking you about some of the exchange students on campus. You will hear each of her questions twice. Answer according to the model, giving the nationality of the persons she mentions and the language they might speak.

MODELO: (¿Evaristo es de Portugal?) → <u>Sí, es portugués y habla portugués.</u>

1. ...   2. ...   3. ...   4. ...

CH. *¿Qué dicen* (are saying) *estas personas?* Use the Spanish equivalent of *this* and *these* and the correct form of an adjective from the following list to tell what these people might be saying. For example, the man in the first drawing might be saying the Spanish equivalent of: This book is large. You will hear a possible answer on the tape. First, listen to the list of adjectives.

1.    2.    3.

4.

5.

corto/a   alto/a   moreno/a   grande   pequeño/a

D. *Entrevista.* You will hear a series of questions. Each will be said twice. Answer according to your own experience. You will hear a possible answer on the tape.

1. ...   2. ...   3. ...   4. ...   5. ...

7. *Expressing Possession and Destination:* Ser *Plus* de; *Contractions* del *and* al

A. *Descripción.* You will hear a series of questions. Each will be said twice. Answer based on the corresponding drawing.

1.

2.

3.

4.

B. *Fotos de un viaje* (trip). You have just returned from a trip to Argentina and are showing your photographs to a friend. Answer her questions about the pictures, using the written cues.

MODELO: (¿Qué es esto?) apartamento / señor Jurado → <u>Es el apartamento del señor Jurado.</u>

1. casa / doctor Vázquez

2. esposo / señora Borges

3. nietos / señores Garza

4. coche / primo de Marta

5. dueño (*owner*) / hotel (*m.*) Princesa   6. patio / casa de mis amigos

C. *¿Adónde regresan mañana?* Tell where these people will return tomorrow, according to their identities. You will hear a possible answer on the tape. First, listen to the list of identities.

médico   dependiente   turista   secretario   estudiante

MODELO: (hospital) → El médico regresa al hospital mañana.

1. ...   2. ...   3. ...   4. ...

CH. *Entrevista.* You will hear a series of questions about yourself, your family, and your activities. Each will be said twice. Answer based on your own experience. No answer will be given on the tape. The word *sus* means "your" in these questions.

1. ...   2. ...   3. ...   4. ...   5. ...

SITUACIONES

Presentaciones

In the following conversations, you will practice handling introductions in Spanish, in informal as well as formal situations. Read the conversations silently, along with the speaker.

En casa...

—Abuelo, quiero presentarle a Adolfo... Adolfo Álvarez Montés. Somos compañeros de clase en la universidad.

—Encantado, don Antonio.

—Igualmente, Adolfo. Bienvenido a nuestra casa.

En clase...

—Profesora, quisiera presentarle a Laura Sánchez Trujillo. Es mi amiga salvadoreña.

—Mucho gusto en conocerla, Laura.

—El gusto es mío, profesora.

En la cafetería...

—Quico, te presento a Adela. Es amiga de Julio, ¿sabes?

—Mucho gusto, Adela.

—Igualmente.

—¿Qué tal si tomamos un café?

—¡De acuerdo!

Now you will participate in two conversations, one in which you are introduced to the parents of one of your friends, and one in which you introduce two of your friends to each other. Choose your responses from the list below. No answer will be given on the tape.

quisiera (quiero) presentarle a...
te presento a...
mucho gusto en conocerlo
mucho gusto en conocerte

1. —Papá, le presento a Kim. Somos compañeras en la clase de español.

   — _mucho gusto en concerte_

   —El gusto es mío, Kim.

2. —Julia, _te presnto a_ .

   —Mucho gusto, Luis.

   —Encantado.

UN POCO DE TODO

A. *Definiciones*. You will hear a series of definitions of family relationships. Each will be said twice. Listen carefully and write the number of the definition next to the word defined. First, listen to the list of words.

_5 4_ mi abuelo _2_   _4_ mi prima

_3_ mi tía   _1_ mi tío

_6_ mi hermano _5_   _2_ mi abuela _6_

B. *Conversación: Hablando de fotos*. You will hear a conversation between two roommates, printed in your manual, about the brother of one of them. Then you will participate in a similar conversation about a sister. Make any necessary changes in the dialogue. You will hear the correct answer on the tape.

—¿Quién es el joven alto y moreno de la foto?

—Es mi hermano Julio.

—¡Qué guapo es!

—¿Te gustaría (*would you like*) conocerlo?

—¡Sí! ¡Claro que sí!

C. *Listening Passage*. You will hear a brief passage about important members of some Hispanic families, *los suegros* (in-laws). It will be read twice. Then you will hear a series of statements about the passage. Circle *C* if the statement is true (*cierto*) or *F* if it is false (*falso*). Answers to this exercise are given at the end of the tape.

   The following words and phrases will appear in the listening passage. Listen to them before the passage is read.

> viven (*they*) *live*
> encontrar *to find*
> ayudan (*they*) *help*
> sus gastos *their expenses*
> el resultado *result*
> juntos *together*

1. C F   2. C F   3. C F   4. C F

CH. *Y para terminar... Descripción: Una reunión familiar.* You will hear a series of questions. Each will be said twice. Answer each question based on the drawing. You will hear a possible answer on the tape.

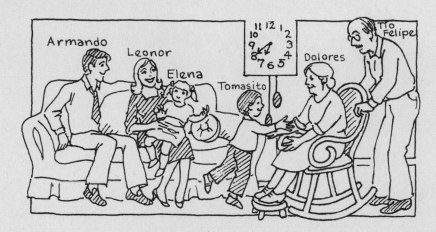

1. ...   2. ...   3. ...   4. ...   5. ...   6. ...

Capítulo 3

PRIMERA PARTE

VOCABULARIO: PREPARACIÓN

A. *Definiciones.* You will hear a series of statements. Each will be said twice. Circle the letter of the phrase defined by each. In this exercise, you will practice listening for the main idea of the sentence. Try not to be distracted by unfamiliar vocabulary.

1. a) grises   b) azules

2. a) pantalones cortos   b) una bolsa

3. a) la corbata   b) la cartera

4. a) verde   b) rojo

5. a) la mochila   b) el abrigo

6. a) regatear   b) rojo

7. a) rosado   b) barato

8. a) de cuadros   b) un par

B. *Identificaciones.* Identify the items after you hear the corresponding number. Begin each sentence with *Es un... , Es una... ,* or *Son... .*

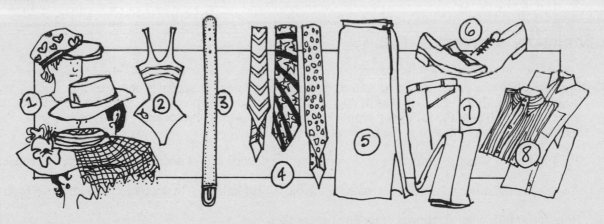

1. ...   2. ...   3. ...   4. ...   5. ...   6. ...   7. ...   8. ...

C. *¿Qué ropa llevan estas personas?* You will hear a series of questions. Answer based on the drawings. You will be describing the clothing these people are wearing and telling who they might be or where they might be. You will hear a possible answer on the tape.

1. ... ...　　2. ... ...　　3. ... ... Están...

CH. *Preguntas.* You will hear a series of questions. Each will be said twice. Answer, using the written cues.

MODELO:　　　　(¿Cuánto pagaste por la radio?) $40,00 → <u>Cuarenta dólares</u>.

1.　$938,00

2.　$159.000,00

3.　33.507

4.　2.432.824

D. *¿De qué color es?* Using tag questions and the written cues, practice asking about the color of the items mentioned on the tape. Use a form of *ser* in each question. You will hear an answer to your questions on the tape.

MODELO:　　　　(la falda) no / rojo → <u>La falda no es roja, ¿verdad?</u>

1.　verde

2.　no / azul

3.　no / anaranjado

4.　blanco

PRONUNCIACIÓN Y ORTOGRAFÍA: D

A. Spanish *d* has two pronunciations. At the beginning of a phrase or sentence and after *n* or *l,* it is pronounced similar to English *d* as in dog. In all other cases, it is pronounced like the English sound *th* in ano*th*er. Repeat the following words and phrases, imitating the speaker. The type of *d* you should be using is indicated at the beginning of each line.

1.　[d] diez　　dos　　doscientos　　doctor　　¿dónde?　　el doctor　　el dinero　　venden

2.　[đ] mucho dinero　　adiós　　usted　　seda　　¿adónde?　　la doctora　　cuadros　　todo

B. Repeat the following sentences, imitating the speaker.

¿Dónde está el dinero?

David Dávila es doctor.

Dos y diez son doce.

¿Qué estudia usted?

Venden de todo, ¿verdad?

C. It is very common in the rapid speech of some Hispanic countries or regions to drop the [d] sound when it appears between two vowels or at the end of a word. Thus, *Jurado* will sound like *Jurao,* and *¿verdad?* will sound like *¿verdá?* Listen to these words.

1. universidad　　libertad　　amistad (*friendship*)

2. lavado (*washed*)　　limpiado (*clean/cleaned*)　　casado　　comprometido (*engaged*)

CH. You will hear a series of words containing the letter *d.* Each will be said twice. Circle the letter of the *d* sound you hear.

1. a)　d　　　　　b) (d̶)
2. a)　d́　　　　　b) (d̶)
3. a) (d)　　　　b)　d̶

4. a)　d̶　　　　　b) (d̶)
5. a)　d　　　　 ˜ b) (d̶)
6. a) (d)　　　　b)　d̶

MINIDIÁLOGOS Y GRAMÁTICA

8. Expressing Actions: Present Tense of -er and -ir Verbs; More About Subject Pronouns

A. *Minidiálogo: Por la tarde, en casa de la familia Robles.* You will hear a dialogue followed by a series of statements. Circle the letter of the name of the person who might have made each statement. In this exercise, you will practice listening for general as well as specific information.

1. a)　el señor Robles　　　　　(b)) la hija
2. (a)) el señor Robles　　　　　(b)) la hija
3. a)　el señor Robles　　　　　(b)) la hija
4. (a)) el señor Robles　　　　　(b)) la hija

B. *Rebajas en el almacén Garrido.* Form sentences using the subject pronouns on tape and cues below. ¡OJO! Remember that subject pronouns are not always used in Spanish.

1. abrir las puertas temprano

2. vender de todo　　Venden de todo

3. ser estupendas　　son estudiadas

4. insistir en ir de compras allí　　insistiamos en ir de compras alli

5. decidir comprar un suéter *decido*

6. insistir en comprar un par de medias *insisto*

C. *¿Qué hacen?* (What are they doing?) Tell what the people in the drawings are doing when you hear the corresponding number. You will hear a possible answer on the tape.

1.

2.

3.

4.

1. ...   2. ...   3. ...   4. ...

CH. *Entrevista.* You will hear a series of questions. Each will be said twice. Answer based on your own experience. No answers will be given on the tape.

1. ...   2. ...   3. ...   4. ...   5. ...

<u>9. *Expressing Actions and States:* tener, venir, preferir, querer, *and* poder; *Some Idioms with* tener</u>

A. *Minidiálogo: No es por falta* (lack) *de ganas...* You will hear a dialogue followed by two statements. Circle the letter of the statement that best summarizes the dialogue. In this exercise, you will practice listening for general information.

1 (2)

B. *Es la semana de exámenes.* Form new sentences, using the oral and written cues. ¡OJO! Remember that subject pronouns are not always used in Spanish.

1. tener muchos exámenes

2. venir a la biblioteca

3. leer cien páginas en dos horas

4. ¡ya no poder leer más!

5. preferir estudiar en la cafetería

6. regresar a la residencia a las diez y media

SEGUNDA PARTE

C. *Situaciones.* Five situations will be described. Each will be read twice. Circle the letter of the expression you associate with each.

1. a) Tengo ganas de regresar a la residencia. b) Tengo prisa.

2. a) Tengo miedo. b) Tengo razón.

3. a) Él no tiene razón. b) Él tiene razón.

4. a) Tengo ganas de trabajar. b) Tengo prisa.

CH. *¿Qué hacemos* (are we doing) *esta noche?* You and your friends are talking about what has to be done and what you would like to do tonight. You will hear each question twice. Answer, using the written cues.

1. Sí,... 4. estar en la cafetería con Tomás

2. mirar la televisión 5. Sí,...

3. Sí,... 6. bailar hasta (*until*) muy tarde

10. Expressing Destination and Future Actions: Ir; ir + a + Infinitive

A. *Minidiálogo: Un regalo para la «mamá» ecuatoriana.* You will hear a dialogue followed by a series of statements about the dialogue. Circle *C* if the statement is true or *F* if it is false. In this exercise, you will practice listening for specific information. The dialogue takes place in Ecuador.

1. C (F) 2. (C) F 3. C (F) 4. (C) F

B. *¿Adónde van después* (after) *de la clase?* Tell where the people listed are going, using the cues you will hear.

1. Francisca
2. nosotros
3. Jorge y Carlos
4. tú
5. la profesora Ruiz

C. *¿Adónde vas?* You will hear a series of sentences about what you like to do or want to do. Using the words listed below, tell where you would go to do these activities, following the model. First, listen to the list of words.

universidad	discoteca	restaurante
almacén	biblioteca	
mercado	farmacia	

MODELO: (Me gusta aprender español.) → <u>Por eso voy a la universidad.</u>

1. ...   2. ...   3. ...   4. ...   5. ...

CH. *Entrevista.* You will hear a series of questions. Each will be said twice. Answer based on your own experience. You will hear a possible answer on the tape.

1. ...   2. ...   3. ...   4. ...   5. ...   6. ...

11. Telling How Long Something Has Been Happening: Hace... que; *Another Use of the Present Tense*

Entrevista. You will hear a series of questions. Each will be said twice. Answer based on your own experience. You will hear a possible answer on the tape.

1. ...   2. ...   3. ...   4. ...   5. ...

SITUACIONES

A. *En una tienda de ropa.* In the following conversation, you will learn about talking to a salesperson about the clothes you are interested in purchasing, as well as the size you wear. Read the dialogue silently, along with the speakers.

—¿Le atienden? ¿Qué desea?

—Hola, buenas. Busco un pantalón de algodón de color oscuro para mí.

—¿Qué talla usa?

—La trece, por lo general.

—¿Qué le parece este pantalón negro?

—No está mal. Y, ¿qué tal una blusa de seda también?

—Cómo no. En su talla tenemos blusas de seda en color beige, rojo y gris perla. Son perfectas para este pantalón.

—¿Dónde me los puedo probar?

—Allí están los probadores. Si necesita algo, mi nombre es Méndez.

—Gracias.

B. *En una zapatería.* Now you will participate in a similar conversation, partially printed in your manual, about buying a pair of shoes. Complete it with information that is true for you. You will hear a possible answer on the tape.

—Buenas tardes, _____ .

—Muy buenas. Busco _____ .

—_____

—_____

—Pues aquí tenemos de todo. _____

—El _____ , por lo general.

—Bueno, tome asiento (*be seated*) mientras le busco unos pares para probar.

UN POCO DE TODO

A. *Buscando regalos para papá.* You will hear a conversation between a brother and sister, who need to buy a birthday gift for their father. Do not be distracted by unfamiliar vocabulary. As you listen, circle the items that they decide to purchase.

B. *Listening Passage.* You will hear a brief passage about a special market in Madrid, Spain. It will be read twice. Then you will hear a series of incomplete statements about the passage. Circle the letter of the phrase that best completes each sentence, based on the passage. Answers to this exercise are given at the end of the tape.

1. a) el Rastro   b) el Rostro

2. a) de todo   b) sólo ropa y comida

3. a) buenos precios   b) precios fijos

4. a) descansar   b) regatear

5. a) ir temprano   b) ir de compras

C. *Hablando de nuestra vida como estudiantes.* You will hear a series of questions. Each will be said twice. Answer based on your own experience. You will hear a possible answer on the tape.

1. ...   2. ...   3. ...   4. ...   5. ...

CH. *Dictado: ¡Qué ganga! Rebajas en el almacén Preciados.* You will hear a conversation between a husband and wife who are shopping at a department store during the sale of the year. Listen carefully and write down the price they paid for each of the following items. In this exercise, you will practice listening for specific information. First, listen to the list of items.

la lámpara: 40.00

el televisor: 70.00

el escritorio con silla: _____

la calculadora: 67.00

el vestido: 82.00

el par de zapatos: 45.000

D. *Y para terminar... Descripción: En casa de la familia Cárdenas.* You will hear a series of questions. Each will be said twice. Answer based on the drawing, imagining that you are a member of the family.

1. ...   2. ...   3. ...   4. ...   5. ...   6. ...

Repaso 1

A. *Conversaciones privadas.* You will overhear a conversation in which two people talk about some of their acquaintances. Then you will hear two sentences in English about the conversation. Circle the number of the statement that best describes the conversation. Try to get the gist of the conversation, and don't worry about unfamiliar vocabulary.

1   2

B. *En el periódico.* You will hear a brief article about a lottery prize won by a group of people in Spain. Listen carefully and circle the numbers you hear. In this exercise, you will practice listening for specific information.

1   2   5   6   8   12   100   10.000   34.000   134.000.000

Now you will hear the article again. Circle the number of the word or words with which you associate the article. Try not to be distracted by unfamiliar vocabulary and see if you can get the gist of the article.

1. los libros

2. la lotería

3. el dinero

4. la policía

C. *¿Dónde están estas personas?* You will hear five brief conversations or parts of conversations. Listen carefully and write the location in which each conversation is taking place next to the number of the conversation. First, listen to the list of possible locations.

una casa   una clase de matemáticas
una biblioteca   una librería
una clase de lenguas   una fiesta estudiantil

1. _____   4. _____

2. _____   5. _____

3. _____

CH. *Dictado: La venta anual.* You will hear an ad for merchandise from a department store. It will be read twice. Listen carefully and write down the requested information. First, listen to the list of new words and expressions that appear in the ad, and the list of information for which you will be listening.

el hogar (*the home*)
vengan a visitarnos (*come visit us*)

el nombre del almacén: _____

el precio de los zapatos para señora: _____

el precio de los trajes para caballero (*men*): _____

tres cosas para el hogar: _____,

_____ , _____

el precio del estéreo: _____

el precio del sofá: _____

D. *Cosas de todos los días.* Practice talking about yourself and others, using the written cues. When you hear the corresponding number, form sentences using the words given in the order given, making any necessary changes and additions. You will hear a possible answer on the tape.

1. yo / llegar / universidad / temprano, / 7:30

2. profesores / llegar / temprano / también

3. Raúl y yo / ir / biblioteca / con frecuencia

4. (nosotros) / estudiar / allí / 2 / hora / todas las noches

5. Raúl / tener / clase / sicología / 11:00 A.M.

6. (ellos) / vender / mucho / cosas / librería

7. yo / ir / librería / antes de (*before*) / mi clase de computación

8. yo / comprar / mochila / nuevo / por (*for*) / $20.00

E. *Conversación: En la facultad.* You will hear a conversation, partially printed in your manual, between two friends who pass each other on campus. Then you will participate in a similar conversation, playing Luisa's role. Answer based on your own experience. No answers will be given on the tape.

ALFREDO: Hola, Luisa. ¿Qué tal?

LUISA: _____

ALFREDO: Así así. ¿Cuándo es el examen en la clase de geografía?

LUISA: _____

ALFREDO: Buena suerte (*luck*), ¿eh? ¿Tienes que trabajar en la librería hoy?

LUISA: _____

ALFREDO: Bueno, hasta luego, Luisa.

LUISA: _____

F. *Descripción: ¿Una familia típica?* You will hear a series of questions about the following cartoon. Each will be said twice. Answer based on your interpretation of the drawing. You will hear a possible answer on tape. First, take time to look at the cartoon and listen to the list of adjectives you may need to answer some of the questions.

bueno   paciente   serio   simpático   malo

1. ...   2. ...   3. ...   4. ...   5. ...   6. ...   7. ...   8. Mi...

G. *Descripción: De compras en el mercado.* You will hear a series of statements about the following drawing. Circle *C* if the statement is true or *F* if it is false. Answer based on the drawing.

1. C F   2. C F   3. C F   4. C F   5. C F

H. *Entrevista.* You will hear a series of questions about yourself. Each will be said twice. Answer based on your own experience. No answers will be given on tape.

1. ...   2. ...   3. ...   4. ...   5. ...   6. ...   7. ...   8. ...   9. ...   10. ...

Capítulo 4

PRIMERA PARTE

VOCABULARIO: PREPARACIÓN

A. *Definiciones.* You will hear a series of statements. Each will be said twice. Circle the letter of the word that is best defined by each statement.

1. a) la luna de miel   b) la amistad

2. a) la boda   b) el divorcio

3. a) cariñoso   b) el novio

4. a) la cita   b) el amor

5. a) el noviazgo   b) el divorcio

B. *Dictado: El horario del profesor Velásquez.* Imagine that you are Professor Velásquez' secretary and that you are filling in her weekly calendar. Listen carefully as she tells you her schedule for this week and fill in the calendar. Some of the entries have already been made.

lunes	martes	miércoles	jueves	viernes
mañana 10:45 AM: _____ Clase de conversación	mañana _____: dentista	mañana _____:	mañana _____:	mañana _____:
tarde _____:	tarde _____:	tarde _____:	tarde 3:00PM: _____ Clase de español	tarde _____:

C. *Conversación: Una cita para esta noche.* You will hear a conversation, partially printed in your manual, about inviting someone to a show. Then you will participate in a similar conversation about another event. Complete it based on the cues suggested. You will hear a possible answer on the tape.

—Oye, tengo dos boletos para _____ esta noche. ¿Quieres _____?

—¡Sí! Hace tiempo que tengo ganas de _____.

—Paso por ti a _____, ¿vale?

—¡De acuerdo!

Here are the cues for your conversation.

la sinfonía
7:45

CH. *¿Dónde están* (are they)? Using this photograph from your recent trip to Colombia, tell a friend where the following things are located in relation to the almacén Sánchez. You will hear a possible answer on the tape. Use prepositions from this list. First, listen to the list.

detrás de	a la izquierda de
delante de	cerca de
a la derecha de	entre

1. la tienda de ropa

2. el mercado

3. el parque

4. la librería

5. el hotel

PRONUNCIACIÓN Y ORTOGRAFÍA: B/V

A. Spanish *b* and *v* are pronounced exactly the same way. At the beginning of a phrase, or after *m* or *n*, *b* and *v* are pronounced like the English b, as a stop; that is, no air is allowed to escape through the lips. In all other positions, *b* and *v* are fricatives; that is, they are produced by allowing some air to escape through the lips. There is no equivalent for this sound in English.

Repeat the following words and phrases, imitating the speaker. Note that the type of *b* sound you will hear is marked at the beginning of the series.

1. [b] bueno   viejo   verde   barato   boda   hombre

2. [b̶] llevar   libro   pobre   abrigo   universidad   abuelo

3. [b/b] bueno / es bueno   busca / Ud. busca   bien / muy bien   en Venezuela / de Venezuela

vende / se vende

4. [b/b] beber   bebida   vivir   biblioteca   Babel   vívido

B. *Repaso:* [d/d] Read the following words and phrases, then listen to the correct pronunciation and repeat.

día domingo Aldo el dinero en Darién

los domingos   todos los días   la verdad

C. *Dictado.* You will hear four sentences. Each will be said twice. Listen carefully and write what you hear.

1. _____

2. _____

3. _____

4. _____

MINIDIÁLOGOS Y GRAMÁTICA

12. *¿Qué estás haciendo?: Estar:* Present Progressive: *Estar + -ndo*

A. *¿Cómo están hoy?* You will hear a series of names and pronouns. Form sentences that tell how each person is feeling today.

MODELO: bien (Ud.) → Ud. está bien.

1. bien   3. enfermo   5. muy bien, ¿verdad?

2. así así   4. enfermo también

B. *El sábado por la tarde: ¿Qué están haciendo estas personas?* Tell what the following people are doing when you hear the corresponding number and the oral cue.

1.

2.

3.

4.

5.

6.

C. *Preguntas*. You will hear a series of questions. Each will be said twice. Answer based on your own experience. You will hear a possible answer on the tape.

1. ...   2. ...   3. ...   4. ...

13. ¿Ser o estar?: Summary of Uses of *ser* and *estar*

A. *Minidiálogo: Una conversación telefónica entre una esposa que está en un viaje de negocios y su esposo que está en casa.* You will hear half of a phone conversation followed by a series of statements about the conversation. Circle the letter of the person who might have made each statement. In this exercise, you will practice listening for specific information. Don't be distracted by unfamiliar vocabulary.

1. a) el esposo   b) la esposa

2. a) el esposo   b) la esposa

3. a) el esposo   b) la esposa

4. a) el esposo   b) la esposa

B. *Marcos, ¿qué tal?* Tell how your friend Marcos seems to be feeling on these different occasions, using one of these adjectives. First, listen to the list of adjectives.

nervioso   furioso   triste   contento   preocupado

1.   2.   3.   4.   5.

C. *¿Quiénes son?* Tell who the people in this family photograph are, using the oral cues.

1. ...   2. ...   3. ...   4. ...   5. ...   6. ...

CH. *¿Ser o estar?* Susana is not sure she has understood what you said. Answer her questions in the affirmative, using *ser* or *estar*, as appropriate.

MODELO: (¿Tú? ¿Muy bien hoy?) → Sí, ¡estoy muy bien hoy!

1. ...   2. ...   3. ...   4. ...   5. ...   6. ...

SEGUNDA PARTE

14. *Expressing Possession: Possessive Adjectives (Unstressed)*

A. *Minidiálogo: En el periódico.* You will hear a letter to *Querida Antonia* and her response, followed by a series of statements. Circle the letter of the person or persons who might have made each statement. In this exercise, you will practice listening for specific and general information.

1. a) Sin Zapatos   b) Antonia   c) los padres de Sin Zapatos

2. a) Sin Zapatos   b) Antonia   c) los padres de Sin Zapatos

3. a) Sin Zapatos   b) Antonia   c) los padres de Sin Zapatos

4. a) Sin Zapatos   b) Antonia   c) los padres de Sin Zapatos

B. *¿Cómo son los parientes de Isabel?* Form new sentences, using the oral and written cues.

MODELO:　　　(familia) grande → <u>Su familia es grande</u>.

1. antipático
2. delgado
3. pequeña
4. viejo
5. muy trabajador

C. *¡Qué confusión!* Sara asks you to clarify what belongs to whom. You will hear each of her questions twice. Answer according to the model.

MODELO:　　　(¿Es la casa de Paco?) → <u>No, no es su casa</u>.

1. ... 　2. ... 　3. ... 　4. ... 　5. ...

CH. *Entrevista.* You will hear a series of questions. Each will be said twice. Answer based on your own experience. No answers will be given on the tape.

1. ... 　2. ... 　3. ... 　4. ... 　5. ...

15. Pointing Out People and Things: Demonstrative Adjectives

A. *Minidiálogo: Delante de una iglesia.* You will hear a dialogue, between a father and his son, followed by a series of statements. Circle the letter of the person who might have made each statement.

1. a) el padre　　　　　　　　　　b) Panchito

2. a) el padre　　　　　　　　　　b) Panchito

3. a) el padre　　　　　　　　　　b) Panchito

4. a) el padre　　　　　　　　　　b) Panchito

B. *¿Cómo son estas cosas?* Answer, using an appropriate form of the indicated demonstrative adjective and the oral cues.

MODELO:　　　ese (falda/azul) → <u>Esa falda es azul</u>.

1. ese　　2. este　　3. aquel　　4. este　　5. ese

C. *Recuerdos de su viaje a México.* Your friends want to know all about your trip to Mexico. Answer their questions, using an appropriate form of the demonstrative adjective *aquel* and the oral cues.

MODELO: ¿Qué tal el restaurante El Charro? (excelente) → ¡Aquel restaurante es excelente!

1. ¿Qué tal el hotel Libertad?

2. ¿Y los dependientes del hotel?

3. ¿Qué tal la ropa en el Mercado de la Merced?

4. ¿Y los periódicos de la capital?

CH. *Dictado: El día de la boda.* You will hear five sentences. Each will be said twice. Write the missing words.

1. _____ señora es la madre del novio y _____ señor es el padre.

2. _____ regalos son para los novios.

3. _____ señorita es la hermana de la novia y _____ mujer es su prima.

4. ¿Y qué es _____? Es el champán para la recepción.

SITUACIONES

A. *Una cita para el fin de semana.* The following dialogue gives examples of how to accept and reject invitations graciously in Spanish, as well as how to extend them. Read the dialogue silently, along with the speakers.

—¡Por fin es viernes! ¡Qué alegría!

—¿Qué vas a hacer este fin de semana?

—El sábado Luisa y yo vamos a la playa, pero regresamos temprano. Ven con nosotros, si quieres.

—Gracias, pero no puedo. Hace tiempo que tengo ganas de ir a la playa, pero tengo varias cosas que hacer mañana. Tal vez otro fin de semana.

—¿Por qué no cenas con nosotros por lo menos? Tenemos mesa en el restaurante La Olla. ¿Sabes dónde está?

—Sí, y es una gran idea. ¿A qué hora?

—Entre las siete menos cuarto y las siete. La mesa está en mi nombre.

—Muy bien y... muchas gracias por insistir. Hasta mañana, ¿eh?

—¡Sí, hasta mañana!

B. Now you will participate in two similar conversations, partially printed in your manual, in which you will accept or decline invitations. Choose your responses from the following list of expressions. In the case of a rejection, be sure to add the reason why you cannot accept the invitation. You will hear a possible answer on the tape. First, listen to the list.

         Gracias, pero tengo que...   sí, ¡claro!
         Lo siento, pero no puedo.   sí, cómo no
         Estoy citado/a con...   ¡estupendo!
         Tengo (que)...   gracias

   1. Después de la clase

       —¿Tienes tiempo ahora para tomar un café?

       — _____

       —Tal vez (*Perhaps*) mañana.

       — _____

   2. Una cita para ir al cine

       —Tengo dos boletos para ir al cine esta noche. ¿Estás libre?

       — _____

       —Y, ¿qué tal si salimos a cenar antes de ir al cine?

       — _____

       —Paso por ti a las siete, ¿de acuerdo?

       — _____

UN POCO DE TODO

A. *En el periódico: Sociales.* You will hear an excerpt from an article printed in the society section of an Hispanic newspaper. Then you will hear two statements about the article. Circle the number of the statement that best summarizes the article.

    1   2

B. *Dictado: Detalles de la boda.* Now the article will be read again. Listen carefully and write down the requested information from the article. First, listen to the information that is requested.

    El día de la semana en que tuvo lugar (*took place*) la boda: _____

    La hora de la boda: _____

    Los nombres de los esposos: _____ y _____

    ¿Hubo (*Was there*) recepción después de la boda? _____

C. *Descripción: Escenas sentimentales.* Describe the following drawings by answering the corresponding questions. You will hear a possible answer on the tape. First, take time to look at each drawing.

1. ver (*to see*)

a. ... b. ... c. ... ch. ... d. ...

2.

a. ... b. ... c. ... ch. ... d. ...

CH. *Listening Passage*. You will hear a brief passage and dialogue about the social implications of invitations in some Hispanic countries. They will be read twice. Then you will hear a series of statements about the passage and dialogue. Circle *C* if the statement is true or *F* if it is false. Answers to this exercise are given at the end of the tape.

The following words and phrases will appear in the listening passage. Listen to them before the passage is read.

la entrada (*ticket*)
cada (*each*)
propia (*own*)

1. C F   2. C F   3. C F

D. *Y para terminar... Entrevista*. You will hear a series of questions. Each will be said twice. Answer based on your own experience. No answers will be given on the tape.

1. ...   2. ...   3. ...   4. ...   5. ...   6. ...

Capítulo 5

PRIMERA PARTE

VOCABULARIO: PREPARACIÓN

A. *¿Qué tiempo hace?* You will hear a series of weather conditions. Each will be said twice. Give the number of the drawing to which each corresponds, then repeat the description. First, look at the drawings.

1.

2.

3.

4.

5.

B. *En el periódico: Hablando del clima.* Look at the following chart of temperatures from a Spanish newspaper from October. Then answer the questions about the chart. You will hear a possible answer on the tape.

First, listen to the list of symbols.

A = agradable

C = mucho calor

c = calor

D = despejado (*clear*)

F = mucho frío

f = frío

H = heladas (*frost*)

N = nevadas

P = lluvioso

Q = cubierto (*cloudy*)

S = tormentas

T = templado (*mild*)

V = vientos fuertes (*strong*)

TEMPERATURAS		MÁX.	MÍN.
Amsterdam	D	12	4
Atenas	D	22	15
Barcelona	D	21	14
Berlín	Q	8	6
Bonn	Q	14	2
Bruselas	D	12	2
Buenos Aires	Q	17	12
Cairo, El	D	26	18
Caracas	D	26	20
Copenhague	D	9	3
Dublin	Q	12	8
Estocolme	f	7	6
Francfort	Q	11	4
Ginebra	Q	13	11
Hamburgo	Q	8	6
Lisboa	D	19	13
Londres	D	13	1
Madrid	A	20	10
México	Q	25	10
Miami	Q	27	23
Moscú	D	2	–6
Múnich	f	8	7
Nueva York	D	19	9
Oslo	f	8	4
Páris	D	13	5
Rabat	Q	23	18
R. de Janeiro	P	25	20
Roma	D	23	15
Tokio	Q	17	12
Viena	Q	12	10
Zúrich	Q	16	9

1. ...   2. ...   3. ...   4. ...   5. ...

C. *Conversación: Gustos y preferencias.* You will hear a conversation, partially printed in your manual, about someone's favorite season. Then you will participate in a similar conversation. Complete it based on your own experience. No answers will be given on the tape.

—De todas las estaciones, ¿cuál es tu favorita?

— _____

— _____ ¿Por qué?

— _____

CH. *¿Cuándo es... ?* Your friend Evangelina wants to know when certain events take place, including a birth date, *una fecha de nacimiento.* Answer, using the written cues.

MODELO: (¿Cuándo es el cumpleaños de Nicolás?) Sunday, May 4 →
            Es el domingo, cuatro de mayo.

1. Friday, August 10

2. Saturday, November 22

3. Wednesday, April 14

4. February 11, 1899

5. July 4, 1776

D. *La ropa y el clima.* You will hear a series of descriptions of what people are wearing at a particular time of year in the U.S. Tell what the weather might be and how each person might be feeling, based on the description. You will hear a possible answer on the tape.

MODELO: (Jorge lleva traje de baño y está en la playa. Es el quince de Julio.) →
            Hace sol y Jorge tiene calor.

1. ...   2. ...   3. ...   4. ...

E. *¿Qué hacemos por la noche?* Form new sentences, using the oral and written cues.

1. Marisol

2. tú

3. los señores Carrasco

4. Vicente y yo

5. yo

6. el profesor de español

F. *Consecuencias lógicas.* You will hear four statements. Each will be said twice. Circle the letter of the phrase that is the logical outcome of that statement. The phrases will not be heard on the tape.

1. a) Por eso hago unas hamburguesas.

    b) Por eso pongo el televisor.

    c) Por eso salgo para la oficina.

2. a) Por eso voy a hacer un viaje a Hawai.

    b) Por eso hago ejercicio.

    c) Por eso hago una pregunta.

3. a) Por eso pongo el aire acondicionador.

    b) Por eso pongo hielo en mi bebida.

    c) Por eso pongo la calefacción.

4. a) Por eso salgo para el cine.

    b) Por eso pongo azúcar en el café.

    c) Por eso salgo con él.

G. *Preguntas personales.* You will hear a series of questions. Each will be said twice. Answer, using the written cues and any other words you need. You will hear a possible answer on the tape.

1. mirar...   a veces visitar a... (*persona*[*s*])

2. salir con...   ir a... (*lugar*)

3. hacer calor

4. 10:30 A.M.   ¡llegar tarde!

PRONUNCIACIÓN Y ORTOGRAFÍA: R *AND* RR

A. The letter *r* has two pronunciations in Spanish: the trilled *r* (written as *rr* between vowels or as *r* at the beginning of a word), and the flap *r,* which appears in all other positions. Because mispronunciations can alter the meaning of a word, it is important to distinguish between these two pronunciations of the Spanish *r.* For example: *coro* (chorus) and *corro* (I run).
    The flap *r* is similar to the sound produced by the rapid pronunciation of *tt* and *dd* in the English words Betty and ladder.

       petty / pero   sadder / Sara   motor / moro

Repeat the following words, phrases, and sentences, imitating the speaker.

1. arte   gracias   pero   vender   triste

2. ruso   Roberto   real   reportero   rebelde

3. burro   corral   carro   barra   corro

4. el nombre correcto   el precio del cuaderno   las residencias   Enrique, Carlos y Rosita

    una mujer refinada   Estos errores son raros.   Puerto Rico   Busco un carro caro.

    el extranjero   Soy el primo de Roque Ramírez.

B. *¿R o rr?* You will hear a series of words. Circle the letter of the word you hear.

1. a) ahora   b) ahorra   4. a) coral   b) corral

2. a) caro   b) carro   5. a) pero   b) perro

3. a) coro   b) corro

C. *Trabalenguas.* You will hear the following Spanish tongue-twister. Listen to it once, then repeat it, imitating the speaker.

    R con R guitarra.

    R con R barril.

    Mira qué rápido corren (*run*)

    los carros del ferrocarril (*railroad*).

MINIDIÁLOGOS Y GRAMÁTICA

16. Expressing Actions: Present Tense of Stem-Changing Verbs

A. *Minidiálogo: Haciendo planes.* You will hear a dialogue followed by a series of statements. Circle the letter of the person who might have made each statement.

1. a) los padres   b) Esteban

2. a) los padres   b) Esteban

3. a) los padres   b) Esteban

4. a) los padres   b) Esteban

B. *Es verano y hace buen tiempo.* ¿Cuáles son las actividades de todos? Form new sentences, using the oral cues.

1. mi madre   4. yo

2. mi amiga y yo   5. el equipo

3. los niños   6. tú

C. *¿Qué estás haciendo?* You will hear a series of situations. Each will be said twice. Tell what you are doing in each situation, using the present progressive of one of the verbs below. Follow the model. First, listen to the list of verbs.

> jugar al tenis afuera   servir el café
> dormir   cerrar mi libro
> pensar en el examen   volver a casa

MODELO: (Es la noche antes del examen final en la clase de química.) →
                  <u>Estoy pensando en el examen.</u>

1. ...   2. ...   3. ...   4. ...   5. ...

CH. *Entrevista.* You will hear a series of questions. Each will be said twice. Answer, using the *nosotros* form of the verbs when appropriate. You will hear a possible answer on the tape.

1. ...   2. ...   3. ...   4. ...   5. ...   6. ...

SEGUNDA PARTE

17. *Describing: Comparisons*

A. *Minidiálogo: Tipos y estereotipos.* You will hear a brief description of the people in the following drawing. Then you will hear a series of statements about them. Circle *C* if the statement is true or *F* if it is false.

1. C F   2. C F   3. C F   4. C F

B. *Un desacuerdo.* You and your friend Lourdes don't agree on anything! React to her statements negatively, following the model.

MODELO: (Esta clase es más importante que aquélla.) →
                      No, esta clase es tan importante como aquélla.

1. ...   2. ...   3. ...   4. ...

C. *Un acuerdo perfecto.* Rafael and Carmen always do and have the same things. Describe their relationship, using the oral cues.

MODELO: (beber / café) → Rafael bebe tanto café como Carmen.

1. ...   2. ...   3. ...   4. ...

CH. *Dictado.* You will hear a series of statements. Each will be said twice. Write the missing words.

1. Esta película es _____ que aquélla. Por eso hay _____ cien personas en

    este cine.

2. Nati tiene _____ hermanos como hermanas. Su hermanito Ángel tiene

    _____ diez años. Es el _____.

3. En el desierto hace _____ calor durante el día que durante la noche. Durante el día, la

    temperatura llega a _____ treinta grados centígrados.

D. *Más descripciones.* You will hear the following sentences, followed by questions. Answer, using a comparison of inequality and the oral cues.

MODELO: Teresa tiene veinte años. (¿Y una persona que tiene cuarenta años?) →
                      Es mayor.

1. Las películas italianas son buenas.

2. Pablo es joven.

3. Comer demasiado (*too much*) es malo.

4. Unas tiendas son grandes.

18. Getting Information: Summary of Interrogative Words

A. *Preguntas y respuestas.* You will hear a series of questions. Each will be said twice. Circle the letter of the best answer to each.

1. a) Es de Juan.   b) Es negro.

2. a) Están en México.   b) Son de México.

3. a) Soy alto y delgado.   b) Bien, gracias. ¿Y Ud.?

4. a) Mañana.   b) Tengo cinco.

5. a) Es gris.   b) Tengo frío.

6. a) Con Elvira.   b) Para comprar chocolates.

7. a) A las nueve.   b) Son las nueve.

B. *¿Qué dijiste?* (What did you say?) Your friend Eva has just made several statements but you haven't understood everything she said. You will hear each statement only once. Choose an appropriate interrogative word and form a question to elicit the information you need.

MODELO: (Llegan mañana.) a) ¿dónde?   b) ¿cuándo? → b - ¿Cuándo llegan?

1. a) ¿de quién?   b) ¿quién?

2. a) ¿quién?   b) ¿quiénes?

3. a) ¿de dónde?   b) ¿adónde?

4. a) ¿cuál?   b) ¿qué?

5. a) ¿cuántos?   b) ¿cuánto?

6. a) ¿a qué hora?   b) ¿qué hora es?

C. *Entrevista con la señorita Moreno.* Interview Ms. Moreno, an exchange student, for your school newspaper, using the written cues. Add any necessary words. You will hear the correct question, as well as her answer.

MODELO: ¿dónde? / ser → Srta. Moreno, ¿de dónde es Ud.? (Soy de Chile.)

1. ¿dónde? / vivir   4. ¿qué? / instrumento

2. ¿dónde? / trabajar   5. ¿cuánto? / hermanos

3. ¿qué? / idiomas

SITUACIONES

A. *Pronóstico del tiempo.* In the following conversation, you will learn some of the vocabulary used in Spanish to talk about the weather, as well as a variety of ways to get information. Read the conversation silently, along with the speakers.

—Oye, ¿sabes qué tiempo va a hacer en San Sebastián la próxima semana?

—Supongo que fresco, pero no estoy seguro. Nunca miro la tele para saber qué tiempo hace. No confío en sus predicciones.

—Fantástico, pero... ¿qué ropa debo llevar? Es la primera vez que voy a San Sebastián. Tú, ¿qué crees?

—En diciembre hace frío en toda España, pero San Sebastián está en la costa.

—¿Y qué?

—Pues que la temperatura es siempre más suave. Lleva una buena chaqueta y un impermeable. Llueve mucho.

—¿Estás seguro? Mira que sólo tengo una hora para hacer la maleta. El tren sale a las siete.

—No te preocupes. En cuanto a las predicciones sobre el tiempo, tengo razón con más frecuencia que la tele.

Más tarde, en el tren, en la radio

«Como ya se comunicó en anteriores servicios informativos, un frente frío de gran intensidad azota las costas del norte. La nieve sigue cayendo en Bilbao y San Sebastián y esta noche se espera que las temperaturas bajarán a un grado bajo cero.»

B. Now you will hear a series of statements about the dialogue. Circle *C* if the statement is true or *F* if it is false.

1. C F   2. C F   3. C F   4. C F

UN POCO DE TODO

A. *Descripción.* Which picture is best described by the sentences you hear? Each will be said twice.

1. a)

b)

2. a)

b)

3. a)

b)

4. a)

b)

5. a)

b)

B. *Listening Passage*. You will hear a brief passage about how the climate affects certain activities in different parts of the Spanish-speaking world. It will be read twice. Then you will hear a series of statements about the passage. Circle *C* if the statement is true or *F* if it is false. Answers to this exercise are given at the end of the tape.

The following words and phrases will appear in the listening passage. Listen to them before the passage is read.

lluviosa (*rainy*)   encontrar (*to find*)
seca (*dry*)   los habitantes (*inhabitants*)

1. C F   2. C F   3. C F   4. C F

C. *Y para terminar... Entrevista*. You will hear a series of questions. Each will be said twice. Answer based on your own experience. You will hear a possible answer on the tape.

1. ...   2. ...   3. ...   4. ...   5. ...   6. ...   7. ...   8. ...

Capítulo 6

PRIMERA PARTE

VOCABULARIO: PREPARACIÓN

A. *¿Qué va a pedir Juan?* Juan and his friend Marta are in a restaurant. Listen to their conversation and circle the items that Juan is going to order.

B. *Identificaciones.* Identify the following foods when you hear the corresponding number. Use the definite article in your answer.

C. *Categorías.* You will hear a series of words. Repeat each word, telling in what category it belongs: *un tipo de carne, un marisco, una fruta, una verdura, un postre,* or *una bebida.*

MODELO: (el té) → <u>El té es una bebida.</u>

1. ...   2. ...   3. ...   4. ...   5. ...   6. ...   7. ...   8. ...

CH. *¿Cuándo comes? ¿Qué comiste ayer?* You will be asked at what time you generally eat your meals and what you ate yesterday at each meal. Each will be said twice. Answer based on your own experience. You will hear a possible answer on the tape.

1. ...   4. Comí...

2. Comí...   5. ...

3. ...   6. Comí...

D. *Para completar.* You will hear a series of incomplete sentences. Each will be said twice. Circle the letter of the statement that best completes each sentence.

1. a) un programa de televisión   b) unas canciones mexicanas

2. a) los postres y la cuenta   b) las palabras

3. a) las flores   b) la música

E. *¡No vamos a volver a ese restaurante!* You and some friends are at a restaurant, and everything is going wrong. Describe what is happening, using the oral and written cues.

1. nosotros   4. yo

2. el camarero   5. el camarero

3. Eva y Ricardo   6. tú

F. *Entrevista.* You will hear a series of questions. Each will be said twice. Answer based on your own experience. No answers will be given on the tape. Note: in question number three, the expression *has comido* means "you have eaten."

1. ...   2. ...   3. ...   4. ...   5. ...   6. ...

PRONUNCIACIÓN Y ORTOGRAFÍA: C, QU

A. The [k] sound in Spanish can be written two ways: before the vowels *a, o,* and *u* it is written as *c;* before *i* and *e,* it is written as *qu.* The letter *k* itself appears only in words that are borrowed from other languages. Unlike the English [k] sound, the Spanish sound is not aspirated; that is, no air is allowed to escape when it is pronounced. Compare the following pairs of English words in which the first [k] sound is aspirated and the second is not.

can / scan   cold / scold   kit / skit

Repeat the following words, imitating the speaker. Remember to pronounce the [k] sound without aspiration.

1. casa   cosa   rico   loca   roca   comida   pescado   camarones

    camarero   cuenta

2. ¿quién?   Quito   aquí   ¿qué?   queso   porque   paquete   quiero

3. kilo   kilogramo   kiosco   kerosén   kilómetro   karate

B. Read the following sentences when you hear the corresponding number. Then repeat each sentence, imitating the speaker. Pay close attention to intonation.

1. ¿Quién quiere comer en casa?

2. ¿De qué color es tu cuarto?

3. El carro que quiere comprar Carlos es muy caro.

C. *Dictado.* You will hear a series of words. Each will be said twice. Listen carefully and write what you hear.

1. _____   4. _____

2. _____   5. _____

3. _____   6. _____

MINIDIÁLOGOS Y GRAMÁTICA

19. Expressing Negation: Indefinite and Negative Words

A. *Descripción.* You will hear a series of questions. Answer according to the drawings.

MODELO:

(¿Hay algo en la pizarra?) → <u>Sí, hay algo en la pizarra. Hay unas palabras.</u>

1.  2.

3.  4.

5.

B. *¡Por eso no come nadie allí!* You will hear a series of questions about a very unpopular restaurant. Each will be said twice. Answer, using the double negative.

MODELO: (¿Sirven algunos postres especiales?) → <u>No, no sirven ningún postre especial</u>.

1. ...   2. ...   3. ...   4. ...

C. *Ningún cumpleaños es perfecto.* Using some of the negative words you have learned and the oral cues, tell someone about your worst birthday.

MODELOS: (cartas) → <u>No hay ninguna carta para mí</u>.
            (bailar) → <u>Nadie quiere bailar conmigo</u>.

1. ...   2. ...   3. ...   4. ...   5. ...

20. *¿Qué sabes y a quién conoces?: Saber and conocer; Personal a*

A. *Minidiálogo: Delante de un restaurante.* You will hear a dialogue followed by a series of statements. Circle the number of the statement that best summarizes the main idea of the dialogue. In this exercise, you will practice listening for the main idea.

1   2   3

B. *¿De veras?* (Really?) You have just made some statements to which your friend Armando reacts with surprise. Respond to his reaction, using *saber* or *conocer,* as appropriate.

MODELO: (¿Tú? ¿jugar al básquetbol?) → <u>Sí, sé jugar muy bien al básquetbol</u>.

1. ...   2. ...   3. ...   4. ...

C. *En un restaurante ruidoso* (noisy). Your friend Margarita has made a series of statements and you haven't quite understood everything she said. Ask her questions based on each statement, using *¿qué?,* *¿a quién?,* or *¿a quiénes?,* as appropriate.

MODELO: (Veo a los señores Garza.) → <u>¿A quiénes ves?</u>

1. ...   2. ...   3. ...   4. ...   5. ...

CH. *Entrevista*. You will hear a series of questions. Each will be said twice. Answer based on your own experience. You will hear a possible answer on the tape.

1. ...   2. ...   3. ...   4. ...   5. ...

SEGUNDA PARTE

21. Expressing What *or* Whom: *Direct Object Pronouns*

A. *Minidiálogo: ¿Dónde vamos a comer?* You will hear a dialogue followed by two statements about the dialogue. Circle the number of the statement that best summarizes what happens in the dialogue. In this dialogue, you will practice listening for the main idea.

1   2

B. *En la cocina* (kitchen). You are preparing a meal, and your friend Pablo is in the kitchen helping you. Answer his questions, using object pronouns and the written cues. You will hear each question twice.

MODELO: (¿Necesitas la olla [*pan*] ahora?)
sí → *¿La olla? Sí, la necesito.*
no → *¿La olla? No, no la necesito todavía.*

1. no   4. no

2. sí   5. sí

3. sí

C. *Descripción: ¿Qué están haciendo estas personas?* You will hear a series of questions. Answer based on the drawings. Follow the model.

MODELO: (¿Está tomando el pedido [*the order*] un camarero?) → *Sí, lo está tomando.*

1. ...   2. ...   3. ...   4. ...

CH. *Entre amigos...* Your friend Manuel, who hasn't seen you for a while, wants to know when the two of you can get together again. Answer his questions, using the written cues. You will hear each question twice.

1. lunes

2. para esta tarde

3. 4:00

4. Café Rocha

D. *Invitaciones.* Some friends of yours want to know when you will invite them to do certain things. Answer according to the model, using the written cues. You will hear each question twice.

MODELO: (¿Cuándo nos invitas a cenar en tu casa?) el sábado → <u>Los invito a cenar el sábado.</u>

1. el jueves

2. el 10 de junio

3. este verano

4. este fin de semana

SITUACIONES

A. *En un restaurante español.* In the following conversation, you will hear how to order from a menu. Read the dialogue silently, along with the speakers.

MANUEL: ¿Nos sentamos? Creo que aquí se está bien.

ANA MARÍA: Perfecto. Aquí viene el camarero. ¿Por qué no pides tú la cena ya que conoces este

restaurante?

CAMARERO: Buenas noches, señores. ¿Desean algo de aperitivo?

MANUEL: Para la señorita, un vermut; para mí, un jerez. Los trae con jamón, queso y anchoas, por favor. ¿Y qué recomienda Ud. de comida?

CAMARERO: El solomillo a la parrilla es la especialidad de la casa. Como plato del día hay paella...

MANUEL: Bueno. De entrada, el gazpacho. De plato fuerte, el solomillo con patatas y guisantes. Ensalada de lechuga y tomate. Y de postre, flan. Vino tinto y, al final, dos cafés.

ANA MARÍA: Manolo, basta ya. ¡Estoy a dieta y he merendado más de la cuenta!

MANUEL: Chica, ¿qué importa? Luego vamos a bailar.

B. *En el restaurante El Charro.* Now the waiter will ask you what you would like to eat. Use the following menu and the written cues to make your choices. You will hear a possible answer on the tape. First, look at the menu.

Menú - El Charro

Antojitos —
Cóctel de camarones
Nachos
Guacamole

Sopas —
Sopa de tortillas
Sopa de pescado

Platos principales —
Mole poblano de guajolote
Tacos "El Charro"
Bistec con papas fritas

Postres —
Helado de chocolate ☆
Flan ☆ Fruta ☆

Bebidas — Vino (tinto, blanco o rosado) ☆ Cerveza ☆
Agua mineral ☆ Café ☆ Té ☆

---

1. Favor de traerme...

2. Me trae... , por favor

3. ¿Todavía hay... ?

4. Entonces, me trae... , por favor

5. Quiero... , por favor

6. Favor de traerme...

UN POCO DE TODO

A. *En el periódico: Guía* (Guide) *de restaurantes.* The following ads for restaurants appeared in a Spanish newspaper. Use them to answer the questions you will hear. Each question will be said twice. First, look at the ads.

1. ...   2. ...   3. ...   4. ...   5. ...

B. *Descripción: Un* picnic *en el parque.* You will hear a series of questions. Each will be said twice. Answer based on the drawing. Use direct object pronouns in your answers, when possible. You will hear a possible answer on the tape.

1. ...   2. ...   3. ...   4. ...   5. ...

C. *Listening Passage.* You will hear a brief passage about the typical bars found in Madrid where *entremeses,* light snacks or hors d'oeuvres are served. The passage will be read twice. Then you will hear a series of incomplete statements about the passage. Complete each statement based on the listening passage. Answers to this exercise are given at the end of the tape.

1. a) tapas   b) tascas

2. a) después de almorzar   b) después de salir del teatro

3. a) bistec con patatas   b) entremeses o tapas

4. a) regatear   b) escuchar música

CH. *Dictado: Un anuncio.* You will hear an ad for a new restaurant that has just opened in town. It will be read twice. Listen carefully and write down the requested information. First, listen to the list of the information that is being requested.

el nombre del restaurante: _____

la dirección (*address*): _____

la especialidad de la casa: _____

otros platos que se sirven allí: _____ , _____

y _____

el horario (*schedule*): _____

¿Se recomienda hacer reservaciones? _____

D. *Y para terminar... Entrevista.* You will hear a series of questions. Each will be said twice. Answer based on your own experience. No answers will be given on the tape.

1. ...   2. ...   3. ...   4. ...   5. ...   6. ...   7. ...   8. ...

Repaso 2

A. *En el periódico: Espectáculos*. You will hear a brief article that appeared in a Spanish newspaper. Then you will hear two statements. Circle the number of the statement that best summarizes the article. In this exercise, you will practice gisting (listening for the main idea).

1   2

B. *De compras con Sergio*. You will hear a paragraph that describes a sequence of events. It will be read twice. Listen carefully and number the drawings in the following series, from 1 to 5, according to the sequence of events described in the paragraph. One of the drawings does not belong at all. Cross it out. First, look at the drawings. In this exercise, you will practice listening for specific information, as well as putting events into the correct sequence.

a.

b.

c.

ch.

d.

e.

C. *Diálogo: Una diferencia de opiniones*. You will hear a conversation between two sisters, Amalia and Margarita. Each has different opinions about love and relationships. The conversation will be followed by a series of statements. Circle *C* if the statement is true or *F* if it is false. Then you will hear a series of questions that ask your thoughts about the same topics. First, listen to the following words and expressions that are used in the conversation.

un trabajo (*job*)   al mismo tiempo (*at the same time*)
enamorada (*in love*)

Diálogo:

1. C F   2. C F   3. C F   4. C F

Opiniones: ...

CH. *Situaciones: Hablando de viajes.* Imagine that you will travel to a variety of places this year. Answer the questions you hear about each of your trips, using the written cues. ¡OJO! The questions may vary slightly from those seen in the model. Change your answers accordingly. You will hear a possible answer on the tape.

MODELO: March 30 / 2 / impermeable
  (¿Cuándo sales para Seattle?) → <u>Salgo el treinta de marzo.</u>
  (¿Cuántas semanas vas a estar allí?) → <u>Creo que dos.</u>
  (¿No llueve mucho en Seattle? → <u>Sí. Por eso voy a llevar mi impermeable.</u>

1. December 15 / 3 / traje de baño

2. February 29 / 1 / camisetas

3. September 1 / 2 / suéteres

D. *Descripción: La boda de Marisol y Gregorio.* Using the written cues, describe what you see in this drawing after you hear the name of each person or item. When more than one choice is given, choose the word that best describes the situation. You will hear a possible answer on the tape.

1. ser / estar   contento / triste

2. llevar   bonito / feo / guapo

3. ser / estar   encima / debajo

4. pedir / servir   el champán

5. ser / estar   tan / más / menos   alto

6. ser / estar   hermano   menor / mayor

E. *En el restaurante La Valenciana.* You are eating lunch, the main meal of the day, in a Spanish restaurant in Madrid. Use the menu below to answer the waiter's questions. Each will be said twice. You will hear a possible answer on the tape. First, listen to the new items on the menu.

Entremeses:
Jamón serrano
Champiñones al ajillo (mushrooms sautéed in garlic)
Calamares fritos (fried squid)

Entradas:
Gazpacho andaluz (cold tomato soup served with condiments)
Ensalada mixta (mixed green salad)
Alcachofas salteadas con jamón (artichokes sautéed with ham)

Platos fuertes:
Solomillo a la parrilla (beef cooked over a grill)
Paella valenciana (rice dish with seafood, chicken, pork & saffron)
Cordero al chilindrón (lamb and red pepper stew)

Postres:
Flan de naranja (orange flan)
Tarta de manzana (apple tart)
Peras al vino (pears in wine)

Bebidas:
Jerez (sherry)   Vino tinto
Té   Vino blanco
Café   Agua mineral

F. *Descripción.* You will hear a series of questions. Each will be said twice. Base your answers on the following cartoon. You will hear a possible answer on the tape.

The following words appear in the questions or are useful for answering them. Listen to them before the questions are read.

    una taza (*cup*)
    veces (*times, occasions*)
    al final (*in the end*)
    por fin (*finally*)

Now look briefly at the cartoon.

1. ... 2. ... 3. ... 4. ... 5. ... 6. ...

G. *Preguntas personales.* You write the gossip column for a newspaper and are assigned to interview a famous personality about his personal life, likes, dislikes, and so on. Formulate the questions you might ask him, using the written cues and an appropriate interrogative word. Add any other necessary words to complete the meaning of your question.

MODELO:　　ser / de → <u>¿De dónde es Ud.?</u>

1. vivir (*lugar*)

2. ser (*descripción*)

3. ser / color favorito

4. ir / esta noche

5. vivir con (*persona*)

H. *Entrevista.* You will hear a series of questions. Each will be said twice. Answer based on your own experience. No answers will be given on the tape.

1. ... 2. ... 3. ... 4. ... 5. ... 6. ... 7. ... 8. ...

Capítulo 7

PRIMERA PARTE

VOCABULARIO: PREPARACIÓN

A. *Situaciones: De viaje.* You will hear a series of situations. Each will be said twice. Circle the letter of the best solution or response for each.

1. a) Salgo en dos semanas.

   b) Compro un boleto de ida y vuelta.

   c) Compro un boleto de ida.

2. a) ¡Estoy aburrido!

   b) ¡Estoy atrasado!

   c) ¡Estoy cansado!

3. a) Pido un pasaje de primera clase

   b) Bajo del avión.

   c) Viajo en clase turística.

4. a) Pedimos asientos en la clase turística.

   b) Pedimos asientos en la sección de fumar.

   c) Pedimos asientos en la sección de no fumar.

5. a) Puedo viajar cn avión.

   b) Puedo viajar en barco (*boat*).

   c) Puedo viajar en tren.

B. *Identificaciones.* Identify the items after you hear the corresponding number. Begin each sentence with *Es...* or *Son...* and the appropriate indefinite article.

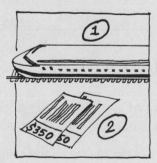

1. ...   2. ...

3. ...   4. ...   5. ...   6. ...   7. ...

C. *Hablando de viajes...* Using the oral and written cues, tell your friend Benito, who has never traveled by plane, the steps one should follow to take an airplane trip.

MODELO: Primero... (llamar a la agencia de viajes) → <u>Primero se llama a la agencia de viajes.</u>

1. pedir

2. El día del viaje,...

3. facturar

4. Después...

5. Cuando anuncian la salida del vuelo,...

6. Por fin...

CH. *Entrevista.* You will hear a series of questions. Each will be said twice. Answer based on your own experience. You will hear a possible answer on the tape.

1. ...   2. ...   3. ...   4. ...   5. ...   6. ...

D. *Conversación: ¡Por fin estamos de vacaciones!* You will hear a conversation, partially printed in your manual, about vacation plans. Then you will participate in a similar conversation about your own vacation plans. Complete it based on your own experience. No answers will be given on the tape.

—¿Cuántos días te dan de vacaciones?

—Este año, _____ .

—¿Vas a ir a algún lugar?

—¡Claro! Voy a _____ con _____ .

PRONUNCIACIÓN Y ORTOGRAFÍA: P, T

A. Like the [k] sound, Spanish [p] and [t] are not aspirated as they are in English. Compare the following pairs of aspirated and nonaspirated English sounds.

   pin / spin   pan / span   tan / Stan   top / stop

Repeat the following words, phrases, and sentences, imitating the speaker.

1. pasar   padre   programa   puerta   esperar

2. tienda   todos   traje   estar   usted

3. una tía trabajadora   tres tristes tigres

   un tío tonto   pasar por la puerta

   unos pantalones pardos   un perro perezoso

4. Tomás toma tu té.   Papá paga el papel.

   También toma tu café.   Pero Pablo paga el periódico.

B. *Repaso: [p], [t], [k]*. You will hear a series of words. Each will be said twice. Circle the letter of the word you hear.

1. a) pata   b) bata   4. a) dos   b) tos

2. a) van   b) pan   5. a) de   b) té

3. a) coma   b) goma   6. a) callo   b) gallo

C. *Dictado: Repaso: p, t, c, and qu*. You will hear four sentences. Each will be said twice. Write what you hear.

1. _____

2. _____

3. _____

4 _____

MINIDIÁLOGOS Y GRAMÁTICA

22. *Expressing to whom or for whom: Indirect Object Pronouns; Dar and decir*

A. *Minidiálogo: En la sala de espera del aeropuerto*. You will hear a dialogue followed by a series of statements. Circle *C* if the statement is true or *F* if it is false. In this exercise, you will practice listening for specific information.

1. C   F   2. C   F   3. C   F   4. C   F

B. *En casa durante la cena.* Practice telling for whom the following things are being done, according to the model.

MODELO: Mi padre sirve el guacamole. (nosotros) → <u>Mi padre *nos* sirve el guacamole.</u>

1. Mi madre sirve la sopa.

2. Ahora ella está preparando la ensalada.

3. Mi hermano trae el café.

4. Rosalinda da postre.

C. *Descripción.* Tell what the people indicated are doing, using the written cues with indirect object pronouns.

En la fiesta de aniversario de los Sres. Moreno

1. Susana: regalar   2. Miguel: mandar   3. Tito: regalar

En casa, durante el desayuno

4. Pedro: dar   5. Marta: dar   6. Luis: servir

CH. *Preguntas.* You will hear a series of questions about things we do for others and things others do for us. Each will be said twice. Answer, using the written cues.

1. hermano menor

2. compañera de cuarto

3. padres

4. hermano menor

5. mejor amigo

6. amigos

23. *Expressing Likes and Dislikes:* Gustar

A. *Descripción: Parece que a Ud. no le gusta el humo* (smoke). You will hear a series of questions. Answer based on the drawing and your own experience. You will hear a possible answer on the tape.

1. ...   2. ...   3. ...   4. ...

B. *¡Vamos de vacaciones! Pero... ¿adónde?* The members of the Soto family can't decide where to go for their vacation. Tell what each person likes, using the oral and written cues.

MODELO: ir a la playa (mi madre / nadar) →
            A mi madre le gusta nadar. Le gustaría ir a la playa.

1. ir a la playa

2. ir a las montañas

3. viajar a Europa

4. quedarse en casa

C. *¿Qué le gusta? ¿Qué odia?* Using the written cues, tell what you like, dislike, or hate about the following situations or locations. You will hear a possible answer on the tape.

MODELOS: En la universidad: fiestas / exámenes →
            Me gustan las fiestas, pero odio los exámenes.
            En una discoteca: la música / las bebidas →
            Me gustan la música y las bebidas.

1. En la playa: sol / nadar

2. En un restaurante: comida / música

3. En un parque: insectos / flores

4. En una pastelería: chocolates / caramelos

CH. *Dictado: Una celebración.* You will hear the following paragraph. It will be read twice. Listen carefully and write the missing words.

Anita y Julio _____ [1] ir a _____ [2] fuera esta noche porque _____ [3]

el cumpleaños de _____ .[4] Anita hace reservaciones en el restaurante _____ [5]

que está cerca de su apartamento _____ [6] es el restaurante favorito de su

_____ .[7] A _____ [8] le _____ [9] mucho la comida mexicana.

Cuando Anita y Julio _____ [10] al restaurante, el camarero _____ [11] enseña la

mesa _____ ,[12] pero no _____ [13] gusta porque está _____ [14] cerca

de la _____ .[15] Por fin encuentran una que _____ [16] _____ [17] situada

y _____ [18] piden el menú _____ [19] camarero. Después de _____ ,[20]

Anita y Julio _____ [21] indican al camarero lo que _____ [22] comer. Él

_____ [23] trae la comida y les dice «¡Buen provecho!» (*"Enjoy your meal!"*)

_____ [24] de cenar, Anita _____ [25] pide dos cafés y _____ [26] de

chocolate _____ [27] camarero. Él _____ [28] trae con la _____ .[29]

Después de _____ ,[30] Anita le pregunta a Julio si le _____ [31] ir a bailar. Para

Julio, fue un _____ [32] muy feliz!

Now you will hear a series of statements based on the preceding paragraph. Each will be said twice. Circle *C* if the statement is true or *F* if it is false.

1. C F   2. C F   3. C F   4. C F   5. C F

SEGUNDA PARTE

D. *Entrevista: Gustos y preferencias.* You will hear a series of questions. Each will be said twice. Answer based on your own experience. No answers will be given on the tape.

1. ...   2. ...   3. ...   4. ...   5. ...   6. ...

24. *Influencing Others: Present Subjunctive: An Introduction: Formal Commands*

A. *Minidiálogo: Un pasajero distraído.* You will hear a dialogue followed by a series of statements about the dialogue. Circle *C* if the statement is true or *F* if it is false. In this exercise, you will practice listening for specific information.

1. C   F   2. C   F   3. C   F   4. C   F

B. Repeat the following verb phrases, imitating the speaker.

1. que cante	que cantes	que cantemos	que canten
2. que diga	que digas	que digamos	que digan
3. que pague	que pagues	que paguemos	que paguen
4. que empiece	que empieces	que empecemos	que empiecen
5. que vaya	que vayas	que vayamos	que vayan
6. que duerma	que duermas	que durmamos	que duerman

C. *Antes del viaje: ¿Qué quiere Ud. que hagan estas personas?* You are traveling with a large group of students. Using the oral and written cues, tell each person what you want him or her to do.

MODELO: Jorge (hacer las maletas) → <u>Quiero que Jorge haga las maletas</u>.

1. Toño

2. Alberto

3. Ana y Teresa

4. todos

5. todos

6. todos

CH. *Consejos y mandatos.* You will hear a series of situations followed by questions. Each will be said twice. Answer each, using an appropriate command based on phrases from the following list. You will hear a possible answer on the tape. First, listen to the list.

(no) acostarse más temprano   (no) fumar aquí
(no) comer tantos postres   (no) viajar en avión
(no) llamarlos   (no) hablar en español

MODELO: (La señorita Alonso es profesora de español. ¿Qué les aconseja ella a los estudiantes de su clase?) → <u>Hablen Uds. en español</u>.

1. ...   2. ...   3. ...   4. ...   5. ...

SITUACIONES

A. *Buscando transporte*. The following conversation shows how to arrange for transportation when traveling by plane. Read it silently, along with the speakers.

En el aeropuerto

—Buenas tardes, señor.

—Muy buenas. Aquí están mi boleto y mi pasaporte.

—Perfecto. ¿Éste es todo el equipaje que va a facturar?

—Sí, sólo esas dos maletas.

—Y ¿dónde quiere sentarse?

—Me gustaría que me ponga en la sección de los no fumadores. Quiero la ventanilla y lo más adelante posible, por favor.

—Muy bien. Tiene el asiento 23A. Ya puede seguir a la puerta de embarque número 7. El vuelo está atrasado veinticinco minutos solamente.

B. Now you will hear another conversation, partially printed in your manual, about arranging for train transportation. Then you will participate in a similar conversation. Complete it with the cues suggested. You will hear a possible answer on the tape.

— _____. Me da _____ .

—¿Para qué tren? Hay un tren a _____, uno a _____ y otro a _____.

—Déme uno para el tren _____.

—Lo siento, pero ya no hay boletos para _____.

—Entonces, _____.

Here are the cues for your conversation:

Panamá-Colón
1:00 P.M.
2:20 P.M.

UN POCO DE TODO

A. *En el periódico: Anuncios*. You will hear an ad for a Mexican airline company. It will be read twice. Then you will hear a series of statements. Circle *C* if the statement is true or *F* if it is false based on the information contained in the ad and the following chart of departures.

MIAMI
10 vuelos semanales

SALIDAS	LUNES 11:50 Y 15:05	MARTES 16:10	MIERCOLES 11:50 Y 16:10	JUEVES 15:15	VIERNES 11:50 Y 11:05	SABADO 15:15	DOMINGO 15:05

1. C F   2. C F   3. C F   4. C F

B. *Anuncios.* You will hear three brief travel ads. Write the number of the ad next to the person or persons who might like the vacation described. First, listen to the description of the persons who are planning their vacations.

_____ *Felipe* es un estudiante y nunca ha viajado a un país extranjero. Para sus vacaciones quiere viajar lejos de su casa, pero no tiene mucho dinero.

_____ *Los Sres. Brown* viven en Alaska y piensan ir de vacaciones en enero porque odian el clima de Alaska durante el invierno.

_____ *Anita y Luisa* son muy deportistas (*sports-minded*) y cada vez que van de vacaciones les gusta ir a lugares que ofrezcan la oportunidad de practicar actividades deportivas.

C. *Listening Passage: Anuncio turístico.* You will hear a brief travel ad. It will be read twice. Then you will hear a series of statements about the passage. Circle *C* if the statement is true or *F* if it is false. Answers to this exercise are given at the end of the tape.

1. C F   2. C F   3. C F   4. C F

CH. *Y para terminar... Descripción: En el avión.* You will hear a series of questions. Each will be said twice. Answer, based on the drawing. You will hear a possible answer on the tape. First, take time to look at the drawing.

1. ...   2. ...   3. ...   4. ...   5. ...   6. ...

Capítulo 8

PRIMERA PARTE

VOCABULARIO: PREPARACIÓN

A. *¿Dónde están?* You will hear a series of conversations or parts of conversations. Write the number of the conversation next to the location in which it might be taking place. First, listen to the list of locations.

_____ una alcoba   _____ un comedor

_____ una sala   _____ un cuarto de baño

_____ una cocina

B. *Hablando de lo que necesitamos.* You will hear a brief dialogue between two friends, Lidia and Daniel. Listen carefully and circle the items that are mentioned in their conversation. Don't be distracted by unfamiliar vocabulary. First, take time to look at the drawing.

C. *Definiciones.* You will hear a series of statements. Each will be said twice. Circle the letter of the word that is best defined by each.

1. a) el trofeo   b) los impuestos

2. a) el grabador de vídeo   b) el compact disc

3. a) la motocicleta   b) la camioneta

4. a) la cámara   b) la cómoda

5. a) el sueldo   b) la alfombra

6. a) el acuario   b) la piscina

CH. *¿Qué hay en esta sala?* You will hear the names of a series of items. Say the number to which each corresponds, then repeat the name. Follow the model.

MODELO: (una mesa) → El número seis es una mesa.

1. ... 2. ... 3. ... 4. ... 5. ...

D. *Entrevista.* You will hear a series of questions. Each will be said twice. Answer based on your own experience. You will hear a possible answer on the tape.

1. ... 2. ... 3. ... 4. ... 5. ...

PRONUNCIACIÓN Y ORTOGRAFÍA: S, Z, Ce, Ci

A. The [s] sound in Spanish can be spelled several different ways and has several variants, depending on the country or region of origin of the speaker. Listen to the difference between these pronunciations of the [s] sound in two distinct Spanish-speaking areas of the world.*

Spain:	Vamos a llamar a Susana este lunes.		
Latin America:	Vamos a llamar a Susana este lunes.		
Spain:	Cecilia siempre cena con Alicia.		
Latin America:	Cecilia siempre cena con Alicia.		
Spain:	Zaragoza	Zurbarán	zapatería
Latin America:	Zaragoza	Zurbarán	zapatería

Notice also that in some parts of the Hispanic world, in rapid speech, the [s] sound becomes aspirated at the end of a syllable or word. Listen as the speaker pronounces these sentences.

¿Hasta cuándo vas a estar allí?

Allí están las mujeres.

Les mandamos las cartas.

Estos niños están sucios.

---

*The Latin American variant of the [s] sound is used by most speakers in this tape program.

B. Repeat the following words and sentences, imitating the speaker.

1. sala   pastel   vaso   sopa   estantes   langostas

2. cocina   piscina   ciudad   sucio   cita   cierto

3. arroz   actriz   azul   razón   perezoso   noviazgo

4. estación   solución   situación   calefacción   contaminación

5. Siempre salgo a cenar con Zoila.

   Ese sitio muy sucio está en esta ciudad.

   No conozco a Luz Mendoza de Pérez.

   Los zapatos de Celia son azules.

C. *Repaso.* You will hear a series of words spelled with *c* or *qu*. Each will be said twice. Circle the letter or letters used to spell each word.

1. c   qu   4. c   qu

2. c   qu   5. c   qu

3. c   qu   6. c   qu

MINIDIÁLOGOS Y GRAMÁTICA

25. *Expressing Desires and Requests: Use of the Subjunctive in Noun Clauses: Influence*

A. *Minidiálogo: El viernes, por la tarde.* You will hear a dialogue followed by three statements. Circle the number of the statement that best summarizes the dialogue. In this exercise, you will practice getting the main idea.

1   2   3

B. *¿Qué recomienda el nuevo jefe?* You have a new boss in your office and he is determined to make some changes. Tell what he recommends, using the written and oral cues.

MODELO: llegar a tiempo: yo (recomendar) → El jefe recomienda que (yo) llegue a tiempo.

1. buscar otro puesto: Ud.

2. trabajar hasta muy tarde: todos

3. dormir en la oficina: Federico

4. ser más puntuales: nosotros

5. traer los contratos: tú

Now you will hear a series of questions about the boss whose requests you have just described. Each will be said twice. Answer based on your own opinions. No answer will be given on the tape.

1. ...   2. ...   3. ...

C. *Preparativos para un viaje en tren*. Your Spanish friends are going on vacation to Germany. They have never been out of the country before. Answer their questions, using object pronouns when possible, but don't try to use both direct and indirect object pronouns in the same sentence. You will hear each question twice.

MODELO: (¿Tenemos que hacer reservaciones?) → <u>Sí, es necesario que las hagan.</u>

1. ...   2. ...   3. ...   4. ...

CH. *Entrevista: Hablando de casas ideales*. Imagine that you have the chance to design your own home. Answer the following questions about the features you would include. Each question will be said twice. You will hear a possible answer on the tape.

1. ...   2. ...   3. ...   4. ...   5. ...

26. *Expressing Feelings: Use of the Subjunctive in Noun Clauses: Emotion*

A. *Minidiálogo: Un futuro peatón*. You will hear a dialogue followed by two statements. Circle the number of the statement that best summarizes the dialogue.

1   2

B. *Sentimientos*. Practice telling how you feel about the following things, using the oral cues. Add any necessary words.

MODELO: no venir nadie a mi fiesta (tener miedo) →
          <u>Tengo miedo de que no venga nadie a mi fiesta.</u>

1. mis padres / estar bien

2. mi auto / no funcionar

3. haber una crisis mundial

4. mis amigos / llamarme con frecuencia

5. tú / no tener trabajo

SEGUNDA PARTE

C. *Comentarios sobre el mundo del trabajo.* Your friend Nuria will make a series of statements, which are printed in your manual. React to her statements, using the oral cues.

MODELO: La jefa va a renunciar a su puesto. (es extraño) →
                  Es extraño que la jefa renuncie a su puesto.

1. Los empleados reciben un buen sueldo.

2. El jefe piensa despedir a Anita.

3. El director hace un viaje a Europa.

4. La abogada (*lawyer*) habla español.

CH. *Descripción: Esperanzas* (hopes) *y temores* (fears). You will hear two questions about each drawing. Answer based on the drawings and the written cues. You will hear a possible answer on the tape.

1. sacar (*to get*) malas notas (*grades*) / sacar una A

2. darle un aumento / despedirla

3. haber regalos para él / no haber nada para él

27. *Expressing Direct and Indirect Objects Together: Double Object Pronouns*

A. *En casa, durante la cena.* Your brother is still hungry and asks about the different foods that might be left. Listen carefully and circle the items to which he is referring.

MODELO: (¿Hay más? Me la pasas, por favor.)

                 (la sopa)   el pan   el pescado

1. las galletas   la fruta   el helado

2. la carne   el postre   los camarones

3. la leche   el vino   las arvejas

4. las papas fritas   la cerveza   el pastel

B. *En el restaurante El Charro.* You will hear a series of questions. Each will be said twice. Answer each based on the drawings. Use double object pronouns in your answers. You will hear a possible answer on the tape.

1. ...   2. ...   3. ...   4. ...

C. *Mandatos de la empresa.* You are the director of a large company and your secretary is asking you if you would like certain things done. You will hear each of his questions twice. Answer, using a formal command and double object pronouns. Follow the written cues.

MODELOS: (¿Quiere que le traiga el diccionario?)
sí → Sí, tráigamelo, por favor.
no → No, no me lo traiga todavía.

1. no   2. sí   3. sí   4. no

CH. *¿Dónde está... ?* Your roommate Carolina would like to borrow some things from you. Tell her to whom you gave each item, using double object pronouns and the written cues. You will hear each of Carolina's questions twice. Note: *di* means "I gave."

MODELO: (Oye, ¿dónde está tu diccionario?) Nicolás / necesitarlo para un examen →
Se lo di a Nicolás. Él lo necesita para un examen.

1. Teresa / tener que estudiar el vocabulario

2. Juan / salir para México mañana

3. Nina / ir a una fiesta el sábado

4. Verónica / tener una cena elegante con su novio esta noche

SITUACIONES

A. *En busca de un cuarto.* In the following conversation, you will hear a description of a place you might want to live. Read the conversation silently, along with the speakers.

—¿Qué te pasa? Pareces muy preocupado.

—Llevo dos semanas buscando cuarto y... ¡nada!

—¿Qué tipo de cuarto buscas?

—Pues... quiero un cuarto para mí solo, que sea grande. Además, necesito muchos estantes para poner libros y un armario bien grande. También me gusta que el cuarto tenga mucha luz y que sea tranquilo.

—¿Nada más?

—Además quiero que esté cerca de la universidad, que tenga garaje, con derecho a usar la cocina, con teléfono... y ¡claro!, que sea barato.

—Hombre, no pides mucho... Pero no te preocupes. Ahora que me lo dices, creo que hay uno en el edificio donde vive Rosario. ¡No sé por qué no se me ocurrió antes! ¿Sabes dónde está?

—Creo que sí. La voy a llamar ahora mismo. Gracias, ¿eh?

B. *Conversación: En busca de vivienda* (housing). Now you will participate in a similar conversation, partially printed in your manual, about looking for an apartment. Complete it based on your own experience. No answers will be given on the tape. You may want to record your answers.

—¿Cuánto tiempo hace que buscas un apartamento?

— _____ .

—Y ¿qué tipo de apartamento quieres?

—Bueno, prefiero que sea un apartamento _____ y que tenga _____ alcoba(s).

También quiero uno con _____. Pero lo que más me importa es que esté

_____ de la universidad.

—¡Buena suerte! Ya sabes que mientras más cerca estés de la universidad, más alto va a ser el

alquiler.

UN POCO DE TODO

A. *El mundo laboral.* You will hear a dialogue followed by a series of statements. Circle the letter of the person who might have made each statement.

1. a) el jefe   b) Álvaro

2. a) el jefe   b) Álvaro

3. a) el jefe   b) Álvaro

4. a) el jefe   b) Álvaro

B. *Listening Passage.* The following brief interview with a Spanish businessman points out some of the differences in business hours between the United States and Spain. The interview will be read twice. Then you will hear a series of statements about the interview. Circle *C* if the statement is true or *F* if it is false. Answers to this exercise are given at the end of the tape.

1. C F   2. C F   3. C F   4. C F

C. *Dictado: Cuando me gradúe...* You will hear a conversation between a college campus interviewer for a large corporation and a student interviewee. Listen carefully and write down the requested information. First, listen to the list of information that is being requested. In this exercise, you will practice listening for specific information.

el nombre de la empresa: _____

el nombre del entrevistador: _____

el nombre de la aspirante: _____

lo que estudia la aspirante: _____

la fecha de graduación de la aspirante: _____

CH. *En el periódico: Clasificados.* The following ads appeared in Hispanic newspapers. Decide which item you would most like to purchase and answer the questions. If the ad for the item you wish to purchase does not have the information asked for in the questions, say *No lo dice*. No answers will be given on the tape. First, look at the ad for the item you want to buy.

D. *Y para terminar... Entrevista.* You will hear a series of questions. Each will be said twice. Answer based on your own experience. You will hear a possible answer on the tape.

1. Me gradúo...   2. ...   3. ...   4. ...   5. ...   6. ...

Capítulo 9

PRIMERA PARTE

VOCABULARIO: PREPARACIÓN

A. *Descripción: El apartamento de David y Raúl.* You will hear a series of statements about the following drawing. Each will be said twice. Circle *C* if the statement is true or *F* if it is false. First, look at the drawing.

1. C F   2. C F   3. C F   4. C F   5. C F

Now you will hear a series of questions. Answer based on the preceding drawing and your own experience. Each question will be said twice. You will hear a possible answer on the tape.

1. ...   2. ...   3. ...   4. ...

B. *Definiciones.* You will hear a series of statements. Each will be said twice. Circle the letter of the word that is best defined by each.

1. a) el vecino   b) la dirección   c) la vista

2. a) el despertador   b) el inquilino   c) el alquiler

3. a) la planta baja   b) las afueras   c) el centro

4. a) la vista   b) el despertador   c) el congelador

5. a) la portera   b) el barbero   c) la dueña

C. *Descripción: El sábado en casa de la familia Hernández.* Tell what the following family members are doing, using the oral cues. Base your answers on the drawings. You will hear a possible answer on the tape.

MODELO:

(despertar) → <u>Los hijos despiertan a sus padres.</u>

1.

2.

3.

4.

5.

6.

CH. *¿Para qué sirven estos aparatos domésticos?* Your young friend Joselito wants to know what various appliances do. Answer his questions, using phrases chosen from the following list. You will hear each of his questions twice. First, listen to the list.

lavar la ropa sucia
acondicionar el aire
cocinar la comida
congelar la carne

tostar(ue) el pan
lavar los platos sucios
secar la ropa mojada (*wet*)

MODELO: (¿Para qué sirve el lavaplatos?) → <u>Lava los platos sucios.</u>

1. ...   2. ...   3. ...   4. ...   5. ...

D. *En el periódico: Pisos y apartamentos*. The following housing ads appeared in a Spanish newspaper. Look at the descriptions of the apartments and decide which one you are most interested in. Then answer the questions you will hear. If the ad for the apartment you have chosen doesn't contain the information requested in the questions, say *No lo dice*. No answers will be given on the tape.

1. ...   2. ...   3. ...   4. ...   5. ...   6. ...

E. *Entrevista: Hablando de la vivienda* (housing). You will hear a series of questions. Each will be said twice. Answer based on your own experience. You will hear a possible answer on the tape.

1. ...   2. ...   3. ...   4. ...   5. ...   6. ...

PRONUNCIACIÓN Y ORTOGRAFÍA: J, G, GU

A. The [x] sound can be written as *j* (before all vowels), or as *g*, before *e* and *i*. Its pronunciation varies, depending on the region or country of origin of the speaker. Note the difference in the pronunciation of these words.

España:	Jorge	jueves	gente	álgebra
el Caribe:	Jorge	jueves	gente	álgebra

B. Repeat the following words and phrases, imitating the speaker.

1. Jalisco   jirafa   fijo   extranjero   mujer   joven   viejo   consejera

2. general   generoso   inteligente   geografía   región   religión   sicología

   biología

3. una región geográfica

   una mujer generosa

   un consejero joven

C. The [g] sound is written as *g* before the vowels *a, o,* and *u,* and as *gu* before *e* and *i*. In addition, it has two variants. At the beginning of a word, after a pause, or after *n*, it is pronounced like the *g* in *get*. In all other positions, it has a softer sound produced by allowing some air to escape when it is pronounced. There is no exact equivalent for this second variant in English.

Repeat the following words and sentences, imitating the speaker.

1. [g] grande   tengo   gusto   gracias   guapo   ganga

2. [g̶] amiga   diálogo   pagar   regatear   delgado   el gorila

3. Tengo algunas amigas guatemaltecas.   ¿Cuánto pagaste?

   ¡Qué ganga!   Domingo es guapo y delgado.

CH. *Dictado.* You will hear five sentences. Each will be said twice. Listen carefully and write what you hear.

1. _____

2. _____

3. _____

4. _____

5. _____

MINIDIÁLOGOS Y GRAMÁTICA

28. Expressing -self / -selves: Reflexive Pronouns

A. *Minidiálogo: Un día típico.* You will hear a description of a typical day in the life of Alicia and Miguel. Then you will hear a series of statements about the description. Circle *C* if the statement is true or *F* if it is false.

   1. C F   2. C F   3. C F

B. *¿Qué hacemos cuando hace mucho calor?* Answer the question, using the written and oral cues. ¡OJO! Not all verbs will be reflexive.

1. Lolita

2. Jorge y su esposa

3. yo

4. nosotras

5. tú

C. *Hábitos y costumbres: Todos somos diferentes.* You will hear a series of statements and questions. Each will be said twice. Answer, using the written cues.

MODELO: (Me levanto a las seis y media. ¿Y José?) 7:00 → <u>Se levanta a las siete</u>.

1. noche

2. después

3. sofá

4. impermeable

5. tarde

CH. *Descripción: ¿Qué están haciendo en este momento?* Using the present progressive of the following verbs, tell what each person in the Hernández family is doing at the moment. You will hear a possible answer on the tape. First, listen to the list of verbs.

     ponerse   afeitarse   levantarse
     vestirse   dormir   bañarse

MODELO: (1) → <u>El bebé está durmiendo</u>.

D. *Escenas domésticas.* Miguelito is asking the maid a lot of questions today. You will hear each question twice. Take the part of the maid and answer his questions according to the written cues. Use object pronouns when possible. ¡OJO! Not all verbs will be reflexive.

    MODELO: (¿Tengo que levantarme ahora mismo?) Sí,... →
                       <u>Sí, Miguelito, levántese ahora mismo</u>.

    1. Sí,...   2. Sí,...   3. Sí,...   4. No,...   5. No,...

SEGUNDA PARTE

29. Talking About the Past (1): Preterite of Regular Verbs and of dar, hacer, ir, and ver

A. *Minidiálogo: Un problema con la agencia de empleos.* You will hear a dialogue followed by a series of statements. Circle the letter of the person who might have made each statement.

    1. a) el ama de casa   b) el empleado de la agencia   c) la criada

    2. a) el ama de casa   b) el empleado de la agencia   c) la criada

    3. a) el ama de casa   b) el empleado de la agencia   c) la criada

    4. a) el ama de casa   b) el empleado de la agencia   c) la criada

B. *¿Presente o pretérito?* You will hear a series of conversations or parts of conversations. Listen carefully and determine if the people are talking about the past or the present. Don't be distracted by unfamiliar vocabulary.

1. a) presente   b) pretérito

2. a) presente   b) pretérito

3. a) presente   b) pretérito

4. a) presente   b) pretérito

5. a) presente   b) pretérito

C. *¿Qué pasó ayer?* Describe what the following people did yesterday, using the oral and written cues.

Antes de la fiesta

1. yo   2. mi compañero de cuarto   3. nosotros

Antes del examen de química

4. Nati y yo   5. Diana   6. todos

CH. *El viaje de los Sres. Blanco.* You will hear a series of questions about Mr. and Mrs. Blanco's recent plane trip to Lima, Perú. Answer, using the written cues.

1. 10:50 A.M.   4. 11:00 P.M.

2. fumar   5. hotel

3. leer revistas

D. *Entrevista: Preguntas personales.* You will hear a series of questions. Each will be said twice. Answer based on your own experience. You will hear a possible answer on the tape.

1. ...   2. ...   3. ...   4. ...   5. ...

30. Expressing each other: Reciprocal Actions with Reflexive Pronouns

Descripción: ¿Qué hacen estas personas? Using the written cues, tell what the following pairs of people are doing when you hear the corresponding number. You will be describing reciprocal actions.

SITUACIONES

La rutina cotidiana. In the following conversations, you will hear a description of a daily routine. Read the conversations silently, along with the speakers. Then you will hear two statements about the conversations. Circle the number of the statement that best summarizes the conversations.

1   2

UN POCO DE TODO

A. *En el periódico: Amoblamiento y decoración.* The following ad appeared in an Argentinian newspaper. Listen to the ad. Then, when you hear the corresponding number, guess the meaning of the following words and phrases. Repeat the words and phrases when you hear the correct answer.

1. amoblamientos

2. fecha de entrega

3. poliuretano

4. belleza natural

B. *Listening Passage.* You will hear a brief passage about architecture in the Hispanic world. It will be read twice. Then you will hear a series of statements about the passage. Circle *C* if the statement is true or *F* if it is false. Answers to this exercise are given at the end of the tape.

1. C F   2. C F   3. C F   4. C F

C. *Descripción: En casa de los Delibes.* You will hear a series of statements about the following drawing. Each will be said twice. Circle *C* if the statement is true or *F* if it is false. First, look at the drawing.

1. C F   2. C F   3. C F   4. C F   5. C F   6. C F

CH. *Preguntas: El día de la fiesta.* You will hear a series of questions about a day on which you gave a party. Each will be said twice. Answer based on the written cues.

1. levantarse / bañarse

2. preparar el desayuno / leer el periódico

3. lavar los platos / llevar la basura al garaje

4. hablar con el nuevo empleado / invitarlo a una fiesta

5. preparar los entremeses / dárselos a los invitados

6. irse a casa: todos / mirar la televisión antes de acostarse

D. *Y para terminar... Anuncios: Se venden aparatos domésticos.* You will hear a series of ads for appliances. Each will be said twice. Write the number of the ad next to the appliance described. First, listen to the list of appliances.

_____ un aire acondicionador

_____ un refrigerador

_____ una estufa

_____ una secadora

Repaso 3

A. You will hear five brief conversations or parts of conversations. Write the number of each conversation in the appropriate blank to indicate where it might have taken place. First, listen to the locations.

_____ un restaurante

_____ un avión

_____ la estación del tren

_____ una oficina

_____ la sala de espera de un aeropuerto

B. *¿Qué quieren Uds. que hagan estas personas?* Using the following list of phrases, answer the questions you hear on tape. You and a friend will be telling what you want a series of people to do for both of you. You will hear each question twice. First, listen to the list.

servirnos la comida
mandarnos los contratos
darnos un aumento

no poner la radio a las 11:00 P.M.
llamar a la doctora
arreglar la luz del comedor

MODELO: (¿Qué quieren Uds. que haga el enfermero? [*nurse*]) →
<u>Queremos que llame a la doctora.</u>

1. ...   2. ...   3. ...   4. ...

C. *Descripción: En casa de la familia Ruiz.* You will hear a series of statements about the following drawing. Circle *C* if the statement is true or *F* if it is false. Then you will be asked to describe some of the actions in the drawing. First, look at the drawing.

¿Cierto o falso?

1. C F 2. C F 3. C F 4. C F

Descripción

1.   2.   3.   4.

CH. *Hablando con el corredor de casas* (real-estate agent). You are a real-estate agent and your clients, Mr. and Mrs. Calvo, have some questions about a house that you are going to show them this afternoon. Each question will be said twice. Answer their questions based on the following floor plan. Note: The word *mide* means "measures." You will hear a possible answer on the tape.

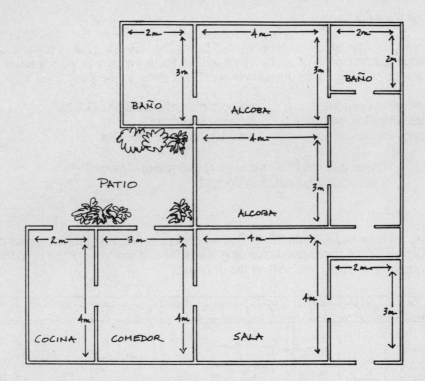

1. ...   2. ...   3. ...   4. ...   5. ...

D. *En busca de vivienda* (housing). You will hear three housing ads. Then you will hear descriptions of people who are looking for housing. Choose the house or apartment that best suits the needs of each person. You may want to jot down notes about the ads and the people in the spaces provided.

Anuncios

Anuncio 1:

Anuncio 2:

Anuncio 3:

Personas

1. los Sres. Robles

2. Maricela y Ricardo

3. Rogelio

E. *Dictado*. You will hear a conversation between a tourist who is interested in traveling to Cancún and a travel agent. The conversation will be read twice. Listen carefully and write down the requested information. First, listen to the list of information that is being requested.

el tipo de boleto que el turista quiere:_____

la fecha de salida: _____

la fecha de regreso (*return*): _____

la sección y la clase en que va a viajar: _____

la ciudad de la cual (*from which*) va a salir el avión: _____

el tipo de hotel que quiere: _____

el nombre del hotel en que se va a quedar: _____

F. *En la agencia de viajes.* Now you will participate in a similar conversation, partially printed in your manual, about making travel reservations. Complete it based on the cues suggested. You will hear a possible answer on the tape.

Here are the cues for your conversation.

> querer / 1 boleto de ida y vuelta / Miami
> April 18 / May 4
> ponerme: Ud. / fumar
> ya tener / reservaciones

—Buenos días. ¿En qué puedo servirle?

—Buenos días. _____ .

—¿Y las fechas de salida y regreso?

—Quiero salir _____ y regresar _____ .

—Muy bien. ¿Prefiere la sección de fumar o la de los no fumadores?

— _____ , por favor.

—Cómo no. ¿Necesita hotel?

—Gracias, pero _____ .

—Muy bien. Aquí tiene su boleto. ¡Buen viaje!

G. *Entrevista.* You will hear a series of questions. Each will be said twice. Answer based on your own experience, using direct and indirect object pronouns whenever possible. No answers will be given on the tape.

1. ... 2. ... 3. ... 4. ... 5. ... 6. ...

Capítulo 10

PRIMERA PARTE

VOCABULARIO: PREPARACIÓN

A. *Días festivos.* You will hear a series of dates. Each will be said twice. Circle the letter of the holiday that is usually celebrated on that date.

1. a) la Noche Vieja   b) la Nochebuena

2. a) el Día de los Muertos   b) el Día del Año Nuevo

3. a) la Navidad   b) la Pascua

4. a) el Día de los Muertos   b) la Noche Vieja

5. a) la Pascua Florida   b) el Día de Gracias

B. *Hablando de ambiciones y carreras.* You will hear three descriptions of people and their careers. Listen carefully and write the name of the person described next to the statement that best summarizes his or her achievements. In this exercise, you will practice listening for specific as well as general information.

_____ llegó a ser director(a) de la compañía.

_____ llegó a ser actor/actriz.

_____ se hizo millonario/a.

C. *¿Cómo reacciona Ud.?* Practice telling how you react to these situations, using the oral and written cues.

MODELO: me olvido del cumpleaños de mi madre (ponerse avergonzado) →
                 <u>Me pongo avergonzada cuando me olvido del cumpleaños de mi madre</u>.

1. mi novio se enoja conmigo

2. mis padres me quitan el coche

3. veo una película triste

4. hablo con mis profesores

5. saco buenas notas

CH. *El mejor restaurante del mundo.* You will hear a series of questions about the "world's best restaurant." Each will be said twice. Answer, using an emphatic form of the indicated adjective or adverb.

MODELO: (¿Qué tal la ensalada?) sabroso → <u>Es sabrosísima</u>.

1. rico   2. bueno   3. caro   4. rápido

D. *Descripción: Una fiesta de la Noche Vieja.* Describe how these people feel or what they are doing, by answering the questions you hear. Each will be said twice. You will hear a possible answer on the tape.

1. ...   2. ...   3. ...   4. ...   5. ...   6. ...

PRONUNCIACIÓN Y ORTOGRAFÍA: Ñ, CH

A. The pronunciation of the *ñ* is similar to the sound [ny] in the English words *canyon* and *union*. However, in Spanish it is pronounced as one single sound.

Repeat the following words and sentences, imitating the speaker.

1. cana / caña   sonar / soñar   mono / moño   tino / tiño   cena / seña

2. año   señora   cañón   español   pequeña   compañero

3. El señor Muñoz es de España.

Los niños pequeños no enseñan español.

La señorita Ordóñez tiene veinte años.

B. You will hear a series of words. Circle the letter of the word you hear.

1. a) pena	b) peña		4. a) suena	b) sueña	
2. a) una	b) uña		5. a) mono	b) moño	
3. a) lena	b) leña				

C. In Spanish, the letter *ch* is pronounced like its English equivalent in *church*. Read the following words when you hear the corresponding number, then repeat the correct pronunciation.

1. mucho
2. muchacho
3. Concha

4. Chile
5. mochila
6. hache

CH. *Dictado.* You will hear four sentences. Each will be said twice. Write what you hear.

1. _____

2. _____

3. _____

4. _____

MINIDIÁLOGOS Y GRAMÁTICA

31. Talking About the Past (2): Irregular Preterites

A. *Minidiálogo: Pronóstico de un nombre.* You will hear a dialogue followed by a series of statements. Circle *C* if the statement is true or *F* if it is false.

1. C F   2. C F   3. C F

B. *Una fiesta de Nochebuena.* Tell what happened at the party, using the oral cues.

1. estar en casa de Mario
2. tener que limpiar la casa
3. venir con comida y regalos

4. cantar villancicos (*Christmas carols*)
5. ¡estar estupenda!

C. *Descripción: ¿Qué hizo Rodolfo hoy?* Tell what Rodolfo did today after you hear the corresponding number for each drawing. Use the verbs and phrases listed. You will hear a possible answer on the tape.

1.  hacer / camas

2.  lavar / ropa

3.  poner / lavaplatos

4. ir / mercado

5. traer / comida a casa

CH. *Preguntas: ¿Qué hiciste la Navidad pasada?* You will hear a series of questions. Each will be said twice. Answer, using the written cues. Use object pronouns when possible.

1. en casa

2. 2 años

3. sí: venir todos mis tíos y primos

4. su novia

5. sí

6. debajo del árbol

32. *Talking about the Past (3): Preterite of Stem-changing Verbs*

A. *La fiesta de despedida de Carmen.* You will hear a brief description of a going-away party for Carmen, narrated by Carmen. Then you will hear a series of questions about the party. Answer them based on the written cues, choosing one verb from each pair.

1. *decidí / decidió* dejar su puesto

2. *organicé / organizaron* una fiesta

3. *empezó / empecé* a llorar

4. *me reí / se rieron* y *hablaron / hablé* hasta las cinco

5. *se sintió / me sentí* un poco triste

B. *¡Qué día más fatal! ¿Qué le pasó a Antonio?* Tell what happened to Antonio when you hear the corresponding number.

1. dormir muy mal anoche

2. despertarse a las cuatro de la mañana

3. no poder desayunar

4. perder el autobús

5. no recordar llevar un reporte

6. tener que regresar a casa

7. llegar muy tarde al trabajo

SEGUNDA PARTE

C. *Entrevistas: En busca de un puesto.* You are an employment counselor. Interview one of the people you counsel, using the oral and written cues. Add any necessary words.

MODELO: (llamar) director → ¿Llamó Ud. al director?

1. empresa   2. solicitud   3. bien   4. puesto

Now play the role of the applicant and answer the counselor's questions in the affirmative or negative, as indicated. Each question will be said twice.

1. No,...   2. Sí,...   3. Sí,...   4. Sí,...

CH. *Entrevista: ¿Qué pasó la semana pasada?* You will hear a series of questions about what happened last week. Each will be said twice. Answer based on your own experience. No answers will be given on the tape.

1. ...   2. ...   3. ...   4. ...   5. ...   6. ...

33. Expressing Extremes: Superlatives

A. *Minidiálogo: Otro aspecto del mundo del trabajo.* You will hear a dialogue followed by a series of statements. Circle the number of the statement that best summarizes the dialogue.

1   2   3

B. *Chismes* (Gossip) *de la boda de Julia y Patricio.* Your friend's wedding celebration has the best of everything. Answer some questions about it, using the written cues.

MODELO: (Son camisas elegantes, ¿verdad?) almacén →
Sí, son las camisas más elegantes del almacén.

1. joyería (*jewelry store*)   4. año

2. fiesta   5. todos los invitados (*guests*)

3. almacén

C. *Entrevista: Opiniones.* You will hear a series of questions. Each will be said twice. Answer based on your own experience and using superlatives. You will hear a possible answer on the tape.

1. ...   2. ...   3. ...   4. ...   5. ...

SITUACIONES

A. *En una fiesta de Navidad.* You will hear a conversation about a Christmas party. Read it silently, along with the speakers.

A la llegada

—¡Chicos, cuánto gusto! ¡Felices Pascuas! Pasen, pasen.

—¡Hola, Antonieta! ¡Felices Pascuas!

—¿Por qué no vino Alejandro?

—Se me olvidó decirte que no pudo regresar. Perdió el vuelo de la tarde.

—Lo siento. Ahora pónganse cómodos y vamos a divertirnos. ¿Qué quieren tomar?

—Una bebida sin alcohol, por favor. Pero, primero, ¿dónde podemos dejar estas cosillas que trajimos?

—¡Ay, muchas gracias! ¡Muy amables! Pueden dejarlas en la cocina. Ahora bien. José Antonio preparó un ponche muy rico que a todos nos gusta.

—Oye, esta fiesta está estupenda. La música es fabulosa y ¡cuánta comida deliciosa!

—¡Pobre Alejandro! Se está perdiendo la mejor fiesta del año.

A la despedida

—Muchas gracias por venir.

—Gracias a ti. ¡Lo pasamos estupendamente!

—Y, como ya te dijimos, mañana vamos a estar aquí a las nueve para ayudarte a limpiar la casa.

—No es necesario que se molesten. Se lo agradezco, de verdad.

—No es molestia.

—Bueno, si insisten... Seguro que entre todos vamos a terminar pronto.

B. Now you will hear another conversation about a holiday, partially printed in your manual. Then you will participate in a similar conversation. Complete it based on your own experience. No answers will be given on the tape.

—¿ _____ ?

—Estuve bailando en casa de unos amigos. Lo pasamos muy bien. ¿Y tú?

— _____ .

—¿Te divertiste?

— _____ .

UN POCO DE TODO

A. *Un día típico.* You will hear a description of a day in Ángela's life, narrated in the past. Then you will hear a series of questions. Answer, based on the description you hear. First, listen to the questions and try to get an idea of the information for which you need to listen.

1. ...   2. ...   3. ...   4. ...   5. ...

B. *¿Qué hiciste ayer?* Using the preterite of the verbs below, tell what you did yesterday. Add any details you need, especially adverbs. No answers will be given on the tape. You may want to record your answers. First, listen to the list of verbs and phrases.

1. despertarse y levantarse a las...

2. apagar el despertador

3. bañarse y vestirse

4. tener tiempo para desayunar

5. llegar...

6. almorzar en...

7. trabajar hasta las...

8. regresar a casa

9. cenar

10. acostarse y dormirse

C. *Listening Passage.* You will hear a brief passage about Carnival celebrations in the Hispanic world. It will be read twice. Then you will hear a series of statements about the passage. Circle *C* if the statement is true or *F* if it is false. Answers to this exercise are given at the end of the tape.

The following words and phrases will appear in the listening passage. Listen to them before the passage is read.

> más conocidas (*best known*)
> temporada (*period of time*)
> la Cuaresma (*Lent*)
> los disfraces (*costumes, disguises*)
> vivos (*bright*)

1. C F   2. C F   3. C F   4. C F

CH. *Y para terminar... Entrevista.* You will hear a series of questions. Each will be said twice. Answer based on your own experience. You will hear a possible answer on the tape.

1. ...   2. ...   3. ...   4. ...   5. ...   6. ...

Capítulo 11

PRIMERA PARTE

VOCABULARIO: PREPARACIÓN

A. *Descripción: ¡Qué día más terrible!* You will hear a series of sentences. Each will be said twice. Write the letter of each sentence next to the appropriate drawing.

1.  —

2.  —

3.  —

4.  —

5.  —

B. *Presiones del trabajo.* You have been under a lot of pressure at work and it is affecting your judgment as well as other aspects of your life. Describe what has happened to you, using the oral cues.

MODELO: (no pagar mis cuentas) → <u>No pagué mis cuentas</u>.

1. ...   2. ...   3. ...   4. ...   5. ...   6. ...

C. *Reacciones.* You will hear a series of situations. React to each, choosing a sentence from the list. First, listen to the list.

> Oye, ¿me puedes prestar tu coche?
> Perdóneme. ¡Fue sin querer!
> ¿Por qué no recoges tus juguetes?
> Profesor, tengo una pregunta.
> Me imagino que te duelen las piernas.
> ¡Qué mala suerte!
> Un frasco (*jar*) de aspirinas, por favor.

MODELO: (A Ud. le duele la cabeza y va a la farmacia. ¿Qué dice Ud.?) →
Un frasco de aspirinas, por favor.

1. ...　2. ...　3. ...　4. ...　5. ...　6. ...

CH. *Una reunión en Barcelona.* Answer the following questions about your business trip to Barcelona, using the oral and written cues.

MODELO: (¿Cuándo salió Ud. para el aeropuerto?) puntual / a las diez →
Salí puntualmente, a las diez.

1. paciente

2. directo

3. inmediato

4. perfecto

5. muy bien

D. *Preguntas personales.* You will hear a series of questions about how you do certain things. Answer, using the written cues or your own information. You will hear a possible answer on the tape. First, listen to the cues.

hablar español	esperar en una cola	salir con mi novio/a
jugar al béisbol	escuchar el estéreo	limpiar la estufa
faltar a clase	tocar el piano	

1. ...　2. ...　3. ...　4. ...　5. ...

E. *Conversación: Hablando de accidentes.* You will hear a brief conversation, printed in your manual, about an accident. Then you will participate in a similar conversation about another accident. Complete it based on the cues suggested. You will hear the correct answer on the tape.

—¿Te hiciste daño en el brazo?

—Sí, me caí por la escalera (*stairs*) y me lo rompí.

—Te duele mucho, ¿verdad?

—Una barbaridad... Ahora no voy a poder jugar en el partido de tenis.

—¡Qué mala suerte! Ojalá que te mejores (*get better*) pronto.

Here are the cues for your conversation.

tropezar con una silla
fútbol

PRONUNCIACIÓN Y ORTOGRAFÍA: Y *and* LL

A. At the beginning of a word or syllable, the Spanish sound *y* is pronounced somewhat like the letter *y* in English *yo-yo* or *papaya*. However, there is no exact English equivalent for this sound. In addition, there are variants of the sound, depending on the country of origin of the speaker.

Listen to these differences:

el Caribe: Yolanda lleva una blusa amarilla. Yo no.
España: Yolanda lleva una blusa amarilla. Yo no.
la Argentina: Yolanda lleva una blusa amarilla. Yo no.

B. Although *y* and *ll* are pronounced exactly the same by most Spanish speakers, in some regions of Spain *ll* is pronounced like the [y] sound in *million,* except that it is one single sound.

Listen to these differences:

España: Guillermo es de Castilla.
Sudamérica: Guillermo es de Castilla.

C. *¿Ll o l?* You will hear a series of words. Each will be said twice. Circle the letter used to spell each.

1. ll   l   4. ll   l

2. ll   l   5. ll   l

3. ll   l   6. ll   l

CH. Repeat the following words, imitating the speaker.

1. llamo   llueve   yogurt   yate   yanqui   yoga

2. ellas   tortilla   millón   mayo   destruyo   tuyo (*yours*)

D. *Repaso: ñ, ll, y.* When you hear the corresponding number, read the following sentences. Then listen to the correct pronunciation and say the sentence again.

1. El señor Muñoz es de España y habla español.

2. Yolanda Carrillo es de Castilla.

3. ¿Llueve o no llueve allá en Yucatán?

MINIDIÁLOGOS Y GRAMÁTICA

34. Descriptions and Habitual Actions in the Past: Imperfect of Regular and Irregular Verbs

A. *Minidiálogo: La nostalgia.* You will hear a dialogue followed by a series of statements about the dialogue. Circle *C* if the statement is true or *F* if it is false.

1. C F   2. C F   3. C F

B. *Describiendo el pasado: En la primaria.* Tell what you and others used to do in grade school, using the oral and written cues.

1. yo

2. Rodolfo

3. tú

4. todos

5. nosotros

C. *¿Qué estaban haciendo ayer en la oficina?* Tell what the following people were doing, using the oral and written cues.

MODELO: la jefa (dar mandatos) → La jefa estaba dando mandatos.

1. Ana y yo...

2. la secretaria...

3. tú...

4. la jefa...

5. todos...

CH. *¿Qué hacían antes?* You will hear a series of sentences about present actions. Tell what used to happen, using the written cues.

MODELO: (Ahora enseña química.) matemáticas → Antes enseñaba matemáticas.

1. California

2. muy mal

3. elegantemente

4. en clase turística

5. mucho

D. *Conversación: Hablando de nuestra niñez* (childhood). You and a group of friends are having a conversation about your childhood. Answer their questions based on your own experience. Each question will be said twice. You will hear two possible answers for each question. Give your own answer, then listen to the possible answers.

1. ...   2. ...   3. ...   4. ...   5. ...

SEGUNDA PARTE

35. *Expressing Unplanned or Unexpected Events: Another Use of* se

A. *Dictado.* You will hear the following sentences. Each will be said twice. Listen carefully and write the missing words.

1. A ellos _____ _____ _____ el número de teléfono de Marta.

2. A Juan _____ _____ _____ los anteojos.

3. No quiero que _____ _____ _____ el equipaje en el aeropuerto.

4. A los niños _____ _____ _____ los juguetes.

B. *¡Qué distraídos estuvimos ayer!* Tell how distracted you and others were yesterday, using the oral and written cues.

1. yo 　　　　　 3. la camarera 　　　　　 5. el niño

2. tú 　　　　　 4. yo

C. *¡Momentos desastrosos!* You will hear a series of statements describing the misfortunes that befell Mr. Cardona recently. Each will be said twice. Restate each sentence, using *se*, according to the model.

MODELO: 　　　(Dejó caer el vaso de cristal.) → Se le cayó el vaso de cristal.

De vacaciones

1. ... 　　2. (quedar)... 　　3. ...

Durante la cena

4. ... 　　5. ... 　　6. (acabar)...

CH. *Descripción: ¿Qué pasó el fin de semana pasado?* You and your friends gave an unsuccessful birthday party. When you hear each name, tell what happened based on the drawing, using *se*. First, look at the drawing.

1. ...
2. ...
3. ...
4. ...
5. ...

D. *Preguntas: ¿Te levantaste con el pie izquierdo?* You will hear a series of questions. Each will be said twice. Answer as if you were a very absent-minded person, using the written cues.

1. tarea para la clase de español

2. coche

3. sí

4. llevar / libros / biblioteca

SITUACIONES

A. *Incidentes de la vida diaria.* You will hear the following brief dialogues that illustrate how to act politely in Spanish in different situations. Read the dialogues silently, along with the speakers.

En una mesa, dondequiera que sea

—¡Oh! Discúlpeme. ¡Qué torpeza! Permítame que le limpie la camisa.

—No se preocupe. No es nada.

—Lo siento muchísimo.

En el autobús o en el metro

—Sígueme. Hay un sitio en el fondo.

—¡Hombre! Es imposible llegar allí.

—¿Tú crees? Mira... Con permiso... disculpe, señora, fue sin querer... Con permiso... Perdone... Permiso, gracias... ¡Uy! Perdón, lo siento, señora.

—¡Maleducado!

Al llegar tarde a una cita

—¡Uf! Lo siento. Créeme que no era mi intención llegar tan tarde. De verdad. Fue culpa del autobús.

—Anda... No te voy a regañar por diez minutos de retraso. No importa.

Al olvidar algo

—Oye, ¿trajiste los apuntes que te pedí?

—¿Los apuntes? ¡Ay! Si ya decía yo que se me olvidaba algo. Se me ha pasado por completo. Lo lamento. Te los llevo el lunes, sin falla.

—Bueno, bueno... No es para tanto.

B. Now you will participate in two conversations, partially printed in your manual. Use expressions from the list below or any others that are appropriate. You will hear a possible answer on the tape. First, listen to the list.

perdón   no se preocupe
¡lo siento!   no te preocupes
fue sin querer   está bien

1. En la farmacia: Ud. tropieza con una señora y a ella se le cae el frasco (*jar*) de medicina que llevaba.

SRA.: ¡Ay, no!... ¡el frasco!

UD.: _____

SRA.: ¿Qué voy a hacer? Esa medicina era para mi hijito, que está enfermo.

UD.: _____ . Yo le compro otro frasco.

2. En el aeropuerto: Ud. se equivoca y toma el asiento de otra persona. Cuando ésta vuelve, quiere que Ud. le dé su puesto.

SR.: Perdón, pero ése es mi asiento.

UD.: _____. Aquí lo tiene.

SR.: Muchas gracias.

UN POCO DE TODO

A. *Situaciones delicadas*. You will hear four situations. Choose the best solution or reaction to each.

1. a) ¡Ay, me hice daño en la mano!

   b) ¡Qué mala suerte, Sr. Ramos! ¿Tiene otro vaso?

   c) Lo siento muchísimo, Sr. Ramos. Fue sin querer. ¿Puedo comprarlo otro?

2. a) No me importa que no te guste el menú, pero vamos a comer aquí.

   b) Lo siento mucho, pero pensé que te gustaría este restaurante. ¿Quieres ir a otro?

   c) Bueno, yo me quedo aquí, pero si tú quieres irte, a mí no me importa.

3. a) Lo siento, viejo, pero no tengo ganas de trabajar más hoy.

   b) Bueno, si Ud. insiste, me quedo a trabajar.

   c) Solamente voy a trabajar tarde si me aumenta el sueldo.

4. a) No se preocupe. Estoy bien.

   b) Mire, señor, si sus niños no dejan de hacer tanto ruido, voy a llamar a la policía.

   c) Por favor, señor, dígale a sus niños que no hagan tanto ruido... ¡Tengo un dolor de cabeza tremendo!

B. *En el periódico: Gente*. You will hear a brief article that appeared in a Spanish newspaper. It will be read twice. Then you will hear a series of statements about the article. Circle *C* if the statement is true or *F* if it is false.

1. C F   2. C F   3. C F   4. C F

C. *Listening Passage.* You will hear a passage and dialogue about a cultural misunderstanding. It will be read twice. Then you will hear a series of statements about the passage and dialogue. Circle *C* if the statement is true or *F* if it is false. Answers to this exercise are given at the end of the tape.

1. C F   2. C F   3. C F   4. C F   5. C F

CH. *Diálogo: Un día terrible...* You will hear a dialogue in which a woman tells her husband what happened to her at the office. Then you will hear a series of questions about the dialogue. Choose the best answer for each. The following words appear in the dialogue. Listen to them before the dialogue is read.

> balance general (*balance sheet*)
> créemelo (tú [*familiar*] *command form of* creer)
> confianzudo/a (*forward, overly familiar*)

Paula, que acaba de llegar a casa
Pedro, su esposo

1. a) Es posible que sea empleada de oficina.

   b) Creo que es directora de una empresa.

2. a) Porque se puso furiosa.

   b) Porque tenía sueño y prisa.

3. a) Porque Paula hizo muchos errores de varios tipos.

   b) Porque Paula se puso muy enojada.

D. *Entrevista.* You will hear a series of questions. Each will be said twice. Answer based on your own experience. No answers will be given on the tape.

1. ...   2. ...   3. ...   4. ...   5. ...   6. ...

E. *Y para terminar... Una canción.* The following song is popular among Spanish university students.

> *Pim-pi-ri-rim-pim-pím*
>
> A mí me gusta el pim-pi-ri-rim-pim-pím
> Con la botella empiná-pa-ra-ra-pa-pá.*   *tilted, raised*
> Con el pim-pi-ri-rim-pim-pím,
> Con el pa-pa-ra-ra-pa-pá.
> Al que no le gusta el vino es un animal,
> Es un animal...
> ...O no tiene un real.*   *coin (money)*

Capítulo 12

PRIMERA PARTE

VOCABULARIO: PREPARACIÓN

A. *¿Cómo se sentía Reinaldo?* You will hear a brief description of how Reinaldo felt last week when he had the flu. Then you will hear the following statements, based on the description, that are out of sequence. Put them in correct sequence, using the numbers 1-5. The first one is done for you.

_____ Por fin fue al médico.

_____ Esta semana se siente mejor.

___1___ El lunes, Reinaldo se despertó con fiebre y dolor de cabeza.

_____ En el consultorio del médico, éste le dio una receta para un antibiótico.

_____ El martes, se sentía peor; le dolía el cuerpo entero.

B. *Dictado: ¿Cómo se sentía Reinaldo la semana pasada?* You will hear the description of Reinaldo's illness again. It will be said only once. Listen carefully and write the missing words.

Estuve _____ _____ la semana pasada. El lunes, cuando me desperté,

_____ _____ y _____ _____ la cabeza. También estaba

un poco _____ y no podía _____ bien. El martes _____ a

_____, pero _____ _____ fue que me dolía _____ el

_____. Por fin _____ una cita con el _____ para el miércoles y él

_____ _____ un _____. Desafortunadamente, _____

que _____ _____ por tres días y _____ al trabajo el resto de la

_____. Como no tenía apetito, no _____ _____ y perdí tres o cuatro

libras. _____ semana, gracias a Dios, _____ _____

_____. ¡Espero que no me vuelva a _____ este año!

C. *Más partes del cuerpo.* Identify the following body parts when you hear the corresponding number. Use *ser* and the appropriate form of the definite article.

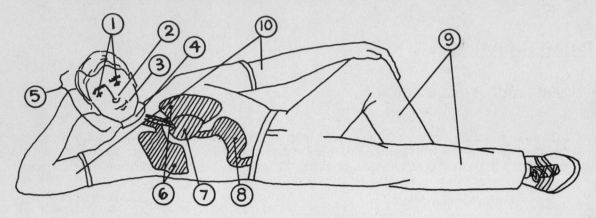

1. ...   2. ...   3. ...   4. ...   5. ...   6. ...   7. ...   8. ...   9. ...   10. ...

CH. *En el consultorio de la doctora Vásquez: ¿Qué debo hacer para estar en buena salud?* You are a doctor whose patient wants to know what he should do to be in good health. Tell him what to do or what *not* to do, using the oral cues. Use formal commands, as in the model.

MODELO: (hacer ejercicio) → Haga Ud. ejercicio.

1. ...   2. ...   3. ...   4. ...   5. ...   6. ...

D. *Para completar.* You will hear a series of incomplete statements. Each will be said twice. Circle the letter of the word or phrase that best completes each statement.

1. a) ponerle una inyección   b) respirar bien

2. a) los ojos   b) el corazón

3. a) una tos   b) un jarabe

4. a) las pastillas verdes   b) esta receta para el antibiótico

5. a) frío   b) un resfriado

6. a) sacar la lengua   b) caminar

E. *Entrevista: Hablando de la salud y el bienestar físico.* You will hear a series of questions. Each will be said twice. Answer based on your own experience. You will hear a possible answer on the tape.

1. ...   2. ...   3. ...   4. ...   5. ...

F. *En el periódico: La salud.* You will hear the following ads from Hispanic newspapers. Listen to them and circle the Spanish words or phrases that express the following. First, listen to the list.

Deje de fumar

1. killers

2. medical treatment

3. a drug

Lentes de contacto

4. a replacement pair

5. immediate replacement

6. soft or flexible

PRONUNCIACIÓN Y ORTOGRAFÍA: X, N

A. The letter *x* is usually pronounced [ks] as in English. Before a consonant, however, it is often pronounced [s]. Repeat the following words, imitating the speaker.

1. [ks] léxico   sexo   axial   existen   examen

2. [s] explican   extraordinario   extremo   sexto   extraterrestre

3. ¿Piensas que existen los extraterrestres?

   ¡Nos explican que es algo extraordinario!

   No me gustan las temperaturas extremas.

   La medicina no es una ciencia exacta.

B. Before *p, b, v,* and *n,* the letter *n* is pronounced [m]. Before the sounds [k], [g], and [x], *n* is pronounced like the [ng] sound in the English word *sing.* In all other positions, *n* is pronounced as it is in English.

Repeat the following words and phrases, imitating the speaker.

1. [m] convence   un beso   un peso   con Manuel   con Pablo   en Perú

   en Venezuela   en México   son buenos

2. [ng] en casa   en Castilla   un general   son generosos   son jóvenes

   en Quito   en Granada   con Juan

MINIDIÁLOGOS Y GRAMÁTICA

36. *Narrating in the Past: Using the Preterite and Imperfect*

A. *Minidiálogo: No es para tanto...* You will hear a dialogue followed by a series of statements about the dialogue. Circle *C* if the statement is true or *F* if it is false.

1. C F   2. C F   3. C F

B. *¿Un sábado típico?* You will hear a series of sentences that describe a series of events. Form new sentences, using the written cues. Begin each sentence with *El sábado pasado...*

MODELO: (Todos los sábados, Carlos se despertaba a las siete.) ocho →
                   El sábado pasado, se despertó a las ocho.

1. mercado

2. café

3. hermana

4. después de la cena

5. tarde

C. *Una decisión difícil.* You will hear the following sentences about Laura's decision to leave her home town. Change the italicized verbs to the preterite or imperfect, according to the oral cues. In this exercise, you will practice narrating in the past.

MODELO: *Vivimos* en un pequeño pueblo en las montañas. (de niños) →
                   De niños, vivíamos en un pequeño pueblo en las montañas.

1. Mi madre *trabaja* en una panadería (*bakery*).

2. Mi padre *trabaja* en una tienda de comestibles (*food store*).

3. *Vamos* a la ciudad y *compramos* cosas que no podemos *encontrar* en nuestro pueblo.

4. *Consigo* trabajo permanente en la ciudad y *decido* dejar mi pueblo para siempre.

5. *Empiezo* a tomar clases de noche en la universidad y *dejo* mi puesto permanente por uno de tiempo parcial.

6. Mis padres *están* tristes porque yo no *vivo* con ellos, pero ahora están contentos con mi decisión.

Now answer the questions you hear based on the preceding story. Each question will be said twice.

1. ...   2. ...   3. ...   4. ...

CH. *Descripción.* Tell what the following people are doing when you hear the corresponding number. Follow the model. You will hear a possible answer on the tape.

MODELO:

mientras → Luis cocinaba mientras Paula ponía la mesa.

1. cuando

2. mientras

3. cuando

4. mientras

5. cuando

SEGUNDA PARTE

D. *Preguntas*. Practice telling how you felt today by answering a series of questions. Each will be said twice. Answer in the affirmative or negative, as indicated by the written cues.

1. sí   2. no   3. sí   4. sí   5. sí

E. *Descripción*. The captions for the following cartoon will be read on the tape. Listen carefully, then answer the questions about the cartoon. You will hear a possible answer on the tape. First, listen to the following expressions that appear in the cartoon.

levantado (*up, out of bed*)
me he sacado de encima (*I got rid of*)
gripe (*flu*)

1. ...   2. ...   3. ...   4. ...   5. ...   6. ...

37. Que, quien, lo que: Relative Pronouns

A. *Minidiálogo: Lo que dijo el Dr. Matamoros.* You will hear a dialogue followed by a series of statements. Circle the letter of the person who might have made each statement.

a) Beatriz	b) su amiga	c) el Dr. Matamoros
a) Beatriz	b) su amiga	c) el Dr. Matamoros
a) Beatriz	b) su amiga	c) el Dr. Matamoros
a) Beatriz	b) su amiga	c) el Dr. Matamoros

B. *Por teléfono.* Tell the receptionist at the hospital with whom you wish to speak, following the model.

MODELO: (el señor Rubio) → El señor Rubio es la persona con quien quiero hablar.

1. ...   2. ...   3. ...   4. ...

C. *En el consultorio.* Imagine that you are Dr. Sotelo. Explain to a nurse what you need and where it is located, following the model.

MODELO: (termómetro) armario → Necesito el termómetro que está en mi armario.

1. mi bolsa   3. mi escritorio

2. mi consultorio   4. ese pueblo

CH. *Problemas de la empresa.* Imagine that you are the director of a company that is experiencing some difficulties. Using the oral cues, tell what you need to improve the situation.

MODELO: (más contratos) → Lo que necesito son más contratos.

1. ...   2. ...   3. ...   4. ...

SITUACIONES

A. *En el consultorio del médico.* In the following dialogues, you will hear conversations between a patient and a nurse and a doctor. Read the dialogues silently, along with the speakers.

Hablando con la enfermera

—Siéntese, por favor. ¿Cómo se llama?

—Tomás Hernández Rodríguez.

—¿Qué es lo que tiene?

—Un resfriado muy grave.

—¿Cuándo empezó a sentirse mal?

—Ayer por la noche tenía fiebre. Tosía mucho y me dolía todo el cuerpo. Hoy me siento peor.

—¿Tiene otros síntomas?

—Por suerte, no.

—Dígame su edad, su peso y su estatura, por favor.

—Tengo veintiún años, mido un metro ochenta y cinco y peso ochenta kilos.

—Muy bien. Ahora, lo que voy a hacer es tomarle la temperatura... Hmm... todavía tiene Ud. fiebre: treinta y ocho grados. Súbase la manga derecha, que le voy a tomar la presión.

—¿Todo esto por un resfriado?

—Es rutinario. Ahora pase Ud. al consultorio de la doctora.

Hablando con la doctora

—Siéntese. Saque la lengua. Abra bien la boca y diga: «Aaaaa... ».

—Aaaaaa.

—La garganta está un poco inflamada. Ahora respire profundamente. Diga: «treinta y tres».

—Treinta y tres.

—Bien. Ud. no tiene nada serio en los pulmones.

—Pero toso mucho, doctora. Ya tosía antes de resfriarme.

—Lo que pasa es que fuma demasiado. Ahora calle mientras le ausculto el corazón. Hmm... ¿hace Ud. mucho ejercicio físico?

—Fui campeón de natación en el colegio. Todavía practico varios deportes.

—Bueno, en general, Ud. está en muy buen estado físico.

—¿Y para este resfriado?

—Pues, unas aspirinas y... paciencia. Para su salud en general, deje de fumar. No es necesaria otra receta.

B. Now you will participate in a conversation, partially printed in your manual, about another illness. Complete it based on the cues suggested. No answers will be given on the tape.

Here are the cues for your conversation:

tener fiebre y dolor de cabeza
dolerme la garganta

—¿Es cierto que te sentías mal ayer?

—Sí, _____ .

—Bueno, por lo menos ya estás mejor.

—¡Qué va! Esta mañana todavía _____ .

UN POCO DE TODO

A. *Ciencia y medicina.* You will hear a brief article from a Spanish magazine. Then you will hear two statements. Circle the number of the statement that best summarizes the article.

1   2

B. *Listening Passage.* You will hear a brief passage about traditional or folk medicine. It will be read twice. Then you will hear a series of statements about the passage. Circle *C* if the statement is true or *F* if it is false. Answers to this exercise are given at the end of the tape.

1. C F   2. C F   3. C F   4. C F

C. *En el aeropuerto.* You will hear a story about a family saying goodbye to a son who is going away to school. Then you will hear the following sentences. Complete them based on the story. You will hear a possible answer on the tape.

1. A las cuatro de la tarde, los señores Restrepo (*estar*) en el aeropuerto con su hijo.

2. Gustavo (*ir*) a San José a (*estudiar*) medicina.

3. Gustavo les (*prometer*) a sus padres que les (*ir*) a escribir frecuentemente.

4. Antes de ir al aeropuerto, la madre le (*hacer*) unos pastelitos.

5. Gustavo (*sentirse*) triste cuando (*despegar*) el avión.

CH. *Entrevista: Preguntas personales.* You will hear a series of questions. Each will be said twice. Answer based on your own experience. No answers will be given on the tape.

1. ...   2. ...   3. ...   4. ...   5. ...   6. ...   7. ...   8. ...

D. *Y para terminar... Una canción. Triste estaba el Rey David* is a 15th-century Spanish song written by Alonso de Mudarra.

Triste estaba el Rey David

Triste estaba el Rey David,
Triste y con gran pasión,
Cuando le vinieron nuevas*   *news*
De la muerte de Absalón.*   *son of David*

Cuando le vinieron nuevas
De la muerte de Absalón,
Palabras triste decía,
Salidas del corazón.*   Salidas... Que venían del corazón

Repaso 4

A. *En el periódico.* You will hear a series of headlines. Write the number of each headline next to the section of the newspaper where it belongs. First, listen to the sections.

_____ Economía

_____ Deportes

_____ Ciencia

_____ Política

_____ Tiempo

B. *En la fiesta del Año Nuevo.* When you hear the corresponding number, describe what happened at your friend Mateo's New Year's Eve party. Use the following groups of words in the order given, and add any necessary words. ¡OJO! You will be using preterite and imperfect verb forms.

1. todos / llegar / nueve

2. Lisbet / traer / entremeses / vino

3. Rafael y yo / venir tarde / porque / perdérsenos / dirección / Mateo

4. Mateo / estar / contentísimo / porque / venir / su novia

5. todos / bailar / mientras / Tito / poner / discos

6. ser / tres / cuando / por fin / terminar / fiesta

C. *Situaciones y reacciones.* You will hear a series of situations. Each will be said twice. Using the written cues, tell how you would react to each. You will hear a possible answer on the tape.

MODELO: (Su compañero de cuarto hizo mucho ruido anoche. ¿Cómo reaccionó Ud.?)
enojarse... porque yo... → Me enojé porque yo quería dormir.

1. ponerse... porque yo...

2. quedarse en casa... porque a mí no me gusta...

3. ponerse... porque yo...

4. ponerse... porque lo que yo decía...

CH. *Descripción: Escenas de la vida diaria.* When you hear the corresponding number, tell what the following people were doing when something else happened. Base your answer on the written cues.

MODELO:  → <u>Rita estaba preparando la comida cuando entró Nuria.</u>

preparar / entrar

1.    limpiar / llegar   2.    tomar / entrar

3.    arreglar / caer   4.    bañarse / sonar

D. *La visita anual al consultorio del médico.* Form sentences about a visit to the doctor's office from the doctor's point of view and from the patient's point of view, using the oral and written cues.

El doctor

1. (yo) / recomendarle (Le recomiendo que...)

2. (yo) / recomendarle

3. (yo) / querer

El paciente

4. (yo) / esperar

5. (yo) / querer

6. (yo) / temer

E. *En el periódico: Viajes.* You will hear the following ad from an Argentinian newspaper. Then you will hear a series of statements. Circle *C* if the statement is true or *F* if it is false, according to the ad.

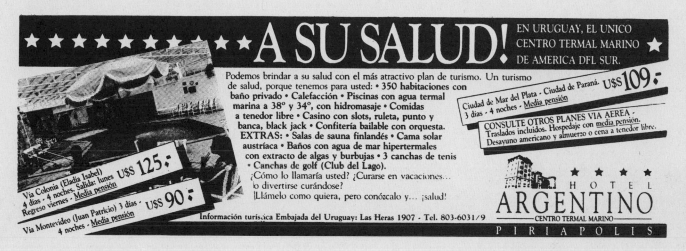

1. C F   2. C F   3. C F   4. C F

F. *Conversación: En el consultorio de la doctora Rubio.* You have been feeling ill for three days. You have a fever, a cough, you feel nauseous. Using these symptoms and any other logical ones, complete the following conversation with Dr. Rubio. No answers will be given on the tape. First, listen to the conversation.

DRA. RUBIO: Buenas tardes. Pase Ud.

UD.: _____.

DRA. RUBIO: Dígame lo que le ocurre, por favor.

UD.: _____

DRA. RUBIO: ¿Y cuánto tiempo hace que se siente así?

UD.: _____

DRA. RUBIO: Bueno, parece que también tiene dificultad con la respiración... ¿Le duelen los pulmones cuando respira?

UD.: _____

DRA. RUBIO: Le voy a dar una receta para un antibiótico y para un jarabe para la tos. Quiero que tome muchos líquidos: agua, té, jugos de fruta... y que descanse. Guarde cama el resto de la semana. Si no está mejor en siete días, llámeme. Hasta luego, y ¡que se mejore pronto!

UD.: _____

G. *Entrevista.* You will hear a series of questions. Each will be said twice. Answer based on your own experience. You will hear a possible answer on the tape.

Hablando de vacaciones

1. ...　　2. ...　　3. ...

Hablando de la salud

4. ...　　5. ...　　6. ...

Hablando de días festivos

7. ...　　8. ...　　9. ...

Capítulo 13

PRIMERA PARTE

VOCABULARIO: PREPARACIÓN

A. *Definiciones: Hablando de coches.* You will hear a series of statements. Each will be said twice. Circle the letter of the word that is best defined by each.

1. a) la batería   b) la gasolina   4. a) la esquina   b) la carretera

2. a) la licencia   b) el camino   5. a) el accidente   b) el taller

3. a) el semáforo   b) los frenos

B. *Identificaciones.* Identify the following items when you hear the corresponding number. Begin each sentence with *Es un...* , *Es una...* , or *Son...*

C. *Descripción.* Answer the questions you hear, based on the preceding drawing. Each question will be said twice. You will hear a possible answer on the tape.

1. ...   2. ...   3. ...   4. ...   5. ...   6. ...

CH. *¿Me puede decir dónde hay una gasolinera?* Someone has just asked you for directions to the nearest gas station. Using *Ud.* command forms, tell her how to get there, using the oral cues.

1. ...   2. ...   3. ...   4. ...

D. *En el periódico: Venta de autos.* The following ads appeared in an Argentinian newspaper. Read them and decide which car you want to buy. Then you will hear a series of questions. Each will be said twice. Answer them according to the ad you chose. No answers will be given on the tape. If the information requested in the question is not in the ad, answer with *No lo dice.*

1. ...

2. ...

3. ...

4. ...

★ M.BENZ 280 CE 1978
Verde, tapizado crema, impec
aire acond, direc hidr antena
eléctrica u$s 16.500
AUTOMOTRICES
ALEMANAS S.R.L.
Av. de Los Incas 5023/29 Cap

RENAULT 18 GTX 84
Una unidad excepcional Para
llevárselo y lucirlo Pocos Km y
buen uso Acepto ptas fac
CORRIENTES 4242
CAPITAL

E. *¿Qué hizo el mecánico?* You will hear a series of car problems. Each will be said twice. Using expressions from the following list, tell what the mechanic did do to fix them. First, listen to the list.

arreglar los frenos   revisar la batería
llenar el tanque   cambiar las llantas

1. ...   2. ...   3. ...   4. ...

F. *Descripción: ¿En qué piso... ?* You will be asked to tell on what floor a number of families live or businesses are located. Each question will be said twice. Answer, based on the following drawing. First, look at the drawing.

1. ...

2. ...

3. ...

4. ...

5. ...

6. ...

7. ...

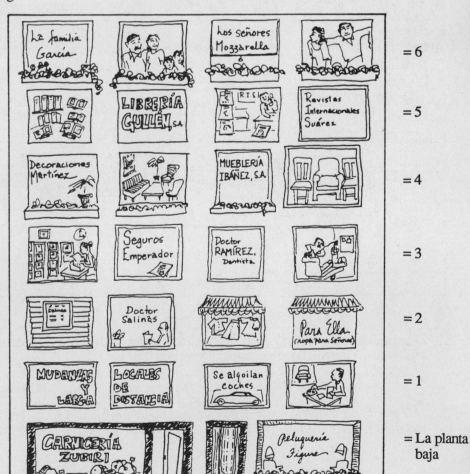

PRONUNCIACIÓN Y ORTOGRAFÍA: *REVIEW OF LINKING*

A. Pronounce the following phrases and sentences as if they were one word.

1. el abuelo   el hijo   el elefante   el otoño

2. los errores   los hoteles   las azafatas   las ideas

3. con Eduardo   son interesantes   en Alemania

4. de usted   para ella   la invitación   mi abuelo

5. mi hijo   me escuchan   la arregló   lo oyó   entre ellos

6. ¿Qué es esto?

Tienen un hijo y una hija.

Aquí hay ocho estudiantes.

Viven así en el Ecuador.

B. *Dictado.* You will hear four sentences. Each will be said twice. Listen carefully and write what you hear.

1. _____

2. _____

3. _____

4. _____

MINIDIÁLOGOS Y GRAMÁTICA

38. *Expressing Uncertainty: Use of the Subjunctive in Noun Clauses: Doubt and Denial*

A. *Comentarios sobre un coche.* You will hear a series of statements about the drawing. Circle *C* if the statement is true or *F* if it is false.

1. C F

2. C F

3. C F

B. *¿Indicativo o subjuntivo?* You will hear a series of sentences. Each will be said twice. Tell whether the sentence expresses certainty (indicative) or doubt (subjunctive).

1. a) certainty   b) doubt   3. a) certainty   b) doubt

2. a) certainty   b) doubt   4. a) certainty   b) doubt

C. *¡Mi coche no funciona!* Practice telling what you should do when your car doesn't work well, using the oral and written cues.

MODELO: Llevo el auto al taller. (Es posible) → Es posible que lleve el auto al taller.

1. Es un auto viejo, pero...

2. El mecánico lo puede arreglar.

3. Sí, pero te cobran (*they'll charge*) mucho.

4. Bueno, puedo manejarlo así, en estas condiciones.

5. Y los frenos funcionan perfectamente.

6. Tienes razón. No debes manejarlo así.

CH. *¿Qué piensa Ud.?* Your friend Josefina has made a series of statements. You will hear each one twice. Respond to each, using the written cues.

MODELO: (Juan trae los contratos.) No creo... → No creo que Juan traiga los contratos.

1. No creo...	3. Dudo...	5. ¡Qué lástima... !
2. Es verdad...	4. Es increíble...	6. No dudo...

D. *De viaje.* Your friend Antonio is very nervous about your upcoming plane trip and is continuously asking you questions. You will hear each question twice. Answer negatively, using object pronouns in your answers, when possible.

MODELO: (¿Crees que Teresa va a perder los boletos?) → No, no creo que los pierda.

1. ... 2. ... 3. ... 4. ...

SEGUNDA PARTE

39. Expressing Influence, Emotion, and Doubt: Uses of the Subjunctive in Noun Clauses: A Summary

A. *Minidiálogo: En el taller.* You will hear a dialogue followed by a series of statements. Circle the letter of the person who might have made each statement.

1. a) cliente   b) empleado   3. a) cliente   b) empleado

2. a) cliente   b) empleado   4. a) cliente   b) empleado

B. *Comprando coche.* Form new sentences, using the oral cues.

1. —¿Qué quiere Ud. que haga el vendedor? (enseñarme los últimos modelos) →
   —<u>Quiero que me enseñe los últimos modelos.</u>

   a. ...   b. ...   c. ...

2. —¿Qué es lo que le sorprende? (costar tanto los coches) →
   —<u>Me sorprende que cuesten tanto los coches.</u>

   a. ...   b. ...   c. ...

C. *Entrevista.* You will hear a series of questions. Each will be said twice. Answer, based on your own experience. No answer will be given on the tape.

1. ...   2. ...   3. ...   4. ...   5. ...

40. *El infinitivo:* Verb + Infinitive; Verb + Preposition + Infinitive

A. *Ventajas y desventajas de la era de la tecnología.* You will hear the following cartoon caption. Then you will hear a series of statements. Circle *C* if the statement is true or *F* if it is false.

1. C F

2. C F

3. C F

—Yo quería ir a su oficina a pagar la tasa de estacionamiento,° pero no pude hacerlo porque no encontré sitio para estacionar.

tasa... *parking fee*

B. *¿Qué hacen sus amigos?* Answer the question, using the oral and written cues.

MODELO: invitarme (salir con ellos) → <u>Me invitan a salir con ellos</u>.

1. ayudarme   2. invitarme   3. insistir   4. tratar

C. *Situaciones.* You will hear a series of situations. Answer, using phrases from the list. ¡OJO! Not all phrases will be used. First, listen to the list.

explicarle lo que pasó
limpiar el parabrisas
ponerles cadenas (*chains*) a las llantas

llevarlo al taller
llamar al médico

1. ...   2. ...   3. ...   4. ...

SITUACIONES

A. *Hablando de coches*. You will hear two dialogues about getting service at a gas station. Read the dialogues silently, along with the speaker.

Un servicio extraordinario

—Buenas. ¿Qué desea?

—Necesito que me arreglen la llanta de repuesto.

—Puede dejarla y pasar mañana a recogerla.

—Pero... es que salgo de viaje ahora mismo... y quisiera tenerla en seguida.

—De acuerdo. Se lo hacemos en diez minutos.

El servicio normal

—Buenos días.

—Buenos días. ¿Le lleno el tanque?

—Sí, primero haga eso, pero después necesito que revise el agua del radiador y el aceite, por favor.

—Sí, cómo no.

—¿En qué puedo servirle?

—Lléneme el tanque, por favor.

—¿Quiere que le revise el aceite?

—Sí, por favor, y el agua de la batería y del radiador. Y otra cosa, ¿podría mirarme la presión de las ruedas?

—De acuerdo. Lleve el coche allí delante. Voy en seguida.

B. Now you will participate in a similar conversation, partially printed in your manual, about asking for service at a gas station. Complete it, based on the cues suggested. You will hear a possible answer on the tape.

Here are the cues for your conversation.

revisarme el aceite   llenarme el tanque   arreglarme la llanta de repuesto

—¿En qué puedo servirle?

—Necesito que Ud. _____ .

—¿Quiere que le mire la presión de las llantas?

—Sí, por favor, y también quiero que _____

y que _____ .

—Sí, cómo no.

UN POCO DE TODO

A. *Se venden coches nuevos y usados*. You will hear three ads for automobiles. Each will be read twice. Listen and complete the following sentences by writing the number of the ad in the appropriate space. First, read the incomplete statements.

Dudo que el coche del anuncio número _____ sea una ganga.

El auto del anuncio número _____ es un auto pequeño y económico.

Es probable que el coche del anuncio número _____ gaste mucha gasolina.

B. *Conversación: Pidiendo información*. You will hear a conversation, partially printed in your manual, about asking for directions. Then you will participate in a similar conversastion about directions to another place. Complete it, based on the cues suggested. No answers will be given on the tape.

—Dígame, por favor, ¿cómo se llega a _____ ?

— _____ . Luego _____ y _____ .

Allí lo va a encontrar.

—Gracias, y perdone la molestia.

— _____ .

Here are the cues for your conversation.

> doblar a la derecha en esta esquina
> seguir todo derecho por la Avenida Santa Ana
> doblar a la izquierda en el primer semáforo
> estar a la izquierda
> de nada

C. *Listening Passage*. You will hear a brief passage about an industry in Latin America. It will be read twice. Then you will hear a series of statements about the passage. Circle *C* if the statement is true or *F* if it is false. Answers to this exercise are given at the end of the tape.

1. C F   2. C F   3. C F   4. C F

CH. *En el extranjero: Se venden y se alquilan coches*. You will hear the following ad. Then you will hear a series of statements about the ad. Circle *C* if the statement is true or *F* if it is false. The following words appear in the ad.

cualquier (*any other*)
fábrica (*factory*)
aduana (*customs duty, fee*)
S.A. (Sociedad Anónima) (*Incorporated* [*Inc.*])

¿VIAJA USTED A ESPAÑA?

COMPRE SU BMW, MERCEDES, VOLVO, VOLKSWAGEN

O cualquier otra marca europea a estricto precio de fábrica.
¡Sin impuestos! ¡Sin aduana! ¡Alquilamos para períodos cortos,
coches nuevos, y tarifas especialísimas!

¡HAGA SU RESERVA YA! ESCRÍBANOS A

REPINTER, S.A.
Capitán Haya, 35. 28020 MADRID. Teléfonos 456 48 08-48 12-48 16

---

1. C F   2. C F   3. C F   4. C F

D. *Entrevista.* You will hear a series of questions. Each will be said twice. Answer, based on your own experience. No answers will be given on the tape.

1. ...   2. ...   3. ...   4. ...   5. ...   6. ...

E. *Y para terminar... Una canción. Cu cu ru cu cu* is a traditional Mexican folk song.

Cu cu ru cu cu

Dicen que por las noches no más se le iba* en puro llorar.	no... pasaba su tiempo
Dicen que no comía, no más se le iba en puro tomar.	
Juran que el mismo cielo se estremecía al oír su llanto.*	Juran... *They swear that even the heavens were touched by his grief.*
Cómo sufría por ella, que hasta en su muerte la fue llamando:	
Ay, ay, ay, ay, ay, cantaba.	
Ay, ay, ay, ay, ay, gemía.*	*he moaned*
Ay, ay, ay, ay, ay, cantaba.	
De pasión mortal moría.	
Cu cu ru cu cu,	
cu cu ru cu cu,	
cu cu ru cu cu.	
Paloma,* ya no le llores.	*Dove*

Capítulo 14

PRIMERA PARTE

VOCABULARIO: PREPARACIÓN

A. *Identificación.* Identify the following objects when you hear the corresponding number. Begin each sentence with the correct form of *ser* and the indefinite article, if needed.

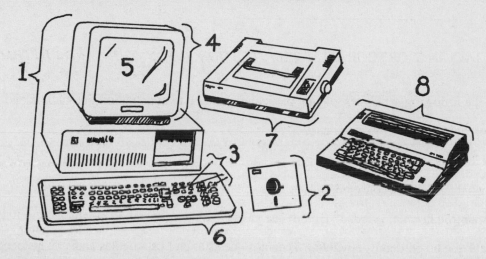

B. *Definiciones.* You will hear a series of statements. Each will be said twice. Choose the word that is best defined by each.

1. a) el inglés   b) el lenguaje   4. a) el técnico   b) el programador

2. a) archivar   b) diseñar   5. a) la informática   b) la pantalla

3. a) la memoria   b) los discos

C. *Diálogo: En la tienda de computadoras.* You will hear a conversation followed by a series of statements. Circle *C* if the statement is true or *F* if it is false. The following words appear in the conversation. Listen to them before the conversation is read.

escritos (*written*)   reparar (*to repair*)
principiantes (*beginners*)   hojas (*sheets* [*of paper*])
aplicaciones (*applications, uses*)

1. C F   2. C F   3. C F   4. C F   5. C F

CH. *¿La ciudad o el campo?* You will hear a series of statements. Each will be said twice. Circle the letter of the location you associate with each.

1. a) la ciudad   b) el campo   4. a) la ciudad   b) el campo

2. a) la ciudad   b) el campo   5. a) la ciudad   b) el campo

3. a) la ciudad   b) el campo   6. a) la ciudad   b) el campo

D. *En el campo.* Imagine that as a child you used to spend your summers in the country. Tell what you used to do, or how you used to feel, using the oral cues.

MODELO: (madrugar todos los días) → <u>Madrugaba todos los días</u>.

1. ...   2. ...   3. ...   4. ...

E. *Gustos y preferencias.* You will hear descriptions of two people, Nicolás and Susana. Then you will hear a series of statements. Write the number of each statement next to the name of the person who might have made it.

Nicolás: _____

Susana: _____

PRONUNCIACIÓN Y ORTOGRAFÍA: *PUNCTUATION, INTONATION, AND RHYTHM*

A. Repeat the following sentences, paying particular attention to punctuation, intonation, and rhythm.

1. ¿Con quién vas a salir esta noche?

2. ¡Es imposible que lo hagamos!

3. ¿Ya hablaste con la consejera?

4. Prepararon la cena, ¿verdad? Espero que ya esté lista porque ¡tengo mucha hambre!

5. Ojalá que no perdamos el vuelo... Tenemos que estar en Los Ángeles antes de las ocho de la noche.

B. *Dictado.* You will hear the following sentences. Each will be said twice. Listen carefully for intonation. Repeat what you hear, then punctuate each sentence.

1. Cuál es tu profesión   Te pagan bien

2. Tú no la conoces verdad

3. Prefiere Ud. que le sirva la comida en el patio

4. Qué ejercicio más fácil

5. No sé dónde viven pero sí sé su número de teléfono

C. When you hear the corresponding number, read the following sentences. Then repeat them, imitating the speaker.

1. Enero es el primer mes del año.

2. No entiendo lo que me estás diciendo.

3. Trabajaba en una tienda donde vendían ordenadores.

4. No olvides el diccionario la próxima vez, ¿eh?

5. Nació (*She was born*) el catorce de abril de mil novecientos sesenta y uno.

6. ¿Adónde crees que vas a ir a estas horas de la noche?

7. Quiero que me ayudes a escribir esta composición.

8. Vamos a llegar al teatro temprano para que no tengamos que hacer cola.

MINIDIÁLOGOS Y GRAMÁTICA

41. *Más descripciones:* Past Participle Used as an Adjective

A. *Consecuencias lógicas.* You will hear a series of sentences that describe actions. Respond to each sentence, telling the probable outcome of the action.

MODELO: (Escribí la composición.) → <u>Ahora la composición está escrita</u>.

1. ...   2. ...   3. ...   4. ...   5. ...

B. *¿Todavía no?* Your friend Marta has been promising to do several things for a long time, but she is a procrastinator. What hasn't she done yet?

MODELO: (Marta me dijo que iba a preparar la cena.) → <u>Sí, pero todavía no está preparada</u>.

1. ...   2. ...   3. ...   4. ...

C. *Entrevista.* You will hear a series of questions. Each will be said twice. Answer, based on your own experience. You will hear a possible answer on the tape.

1. ...   2. ...   3. ...   4. ...   5. ...

42. *¿Qué has hecho?:* Perfect Forms: Present Perfect Indicative and Present Perfect Subjunctive

A. *Minidiálogo: ¿Cambio de ritmo?* You will hear a dialogue followed by a series of statements. Circle the letter of the person who might have made each statement.

1. a) Aurelia   b) Rafael   3. a) Aurelia   b) Rafael

2. a) Aurelia   b) Rafael   4. a) Aurelia   b) Rafael

B. *Un día en la finca: ¿Qué ha pasado ya?* You will hear a series of sentences. Each will be said twice. Circle the letter of the subject of the verb in each sentence.

1. a) yo   b) ella   4. a) nosotros   b) yo

2. a) él   b) nosotros   5. a) ellos   b) él

3. a) nosotros   b) tú

C. *¿Qué hemos hecho hoy?* Form new sentences, using the oral and written cues. Use the present perfect indicative of the verbs.

1. despertarse

2. hacer las camas

3. vestirse

4. desayunar

5. salir para la oficina

SEGUNDA PARTE

CH. *¿Te puedo ayudar?* You have a lot to do before a dinner party and your friend Ernesto wants to know if he can be of help. You appreciate his offer, but you have already done the things he asks about. You will hear each of his questions twice. Answer them according to the model.

MODELO: (¿Quieres que llame a los señores Moreno?) → No, gracias, ya los he llamado.

1. ...   2. ...   3. ...   4. ...   5. ...

D. *Un desacuerdo.* You will hear a brief conversation between two friends, Arturo and Luciano, who disagree on certain environmental issues. It will be read twice. Complete the following sentences, based on their conversation.

1. Arturo cree que las empresas _____ _____ (*ser*) irresponsables.

2. Según Arturo, las empresas _____ _____ (*contaminar*) el medio ambiente.

3. Luciano cree que lo que _____ _____ (*decir*) Arturo no es totalmente cierto.

4. Luciano dice que las empresas _____ _____ (*empezar*) a resolver algunos de los problemas.

E. *Un caso de contaminación ambiental.* Imagine that a case of environmental pollution was discovered earlier this year in your community. Using the oral and written cues, form sentences that express what the residents have said about the incident. Follow the model.

MODELO: ya estudiar el problema (es probable) →
Es probable que ya hayan estudiado el problema.

1. todavía no avisar (*to notify*) a todos los habitantes de la ciudad

2. ya consultar con los expertos

3. descubrir la solución todavía

4. ya resolver el problema

F. *Entrevista.* You will hear a series of questions. Each will be said twice. Answer, based on your own experience. You will hear a possible answer on the tape.

1. ...   2. ...   3. ...   4. ...   5. ...   6. ...

SITUACIONES

A. *Facetas de la ciudad y del campo.* You will hear two dialogues in which the advantages and disadvantages of the city and the country are discussed. Read the dialogues silently, along with the speakers.

Un viaje al campo

—Estoy entusiasmado con este viaje, ¿sabes? Siempre me ha encantado el campo.

—A mí también, pero sólo para los fines de semana. Prefiero estar en la ciudad, donde hay más servicios públicos y posibilidades de trabajo.

—¿Y qué me dices del aire contaminado, el ritmo acelerado de la vida, las viviendas amontonadas, los delitos... ?

—No te los puedo negar. Y si estamos contando todo lo malo, hay que admitir que la ciudad siempre ha explotado al campo y a los campesinos. A éstos se les paga muy poco por las cosechas. Pero en la ciudad hay mejores posibilidades: la educación, los negocios...

Entre la ciudad y el campo

—¿Qué tal el verano en la urbanización? ¿No cambiaste casa con mis primos por un mes?

—Sí, pero Juan Antonio regresó a nuestro piso al cabo de una semana.

—¿Ha pasado algo?

—No, el sitio es verdaderamente ideal y la casa es preciosa. Pero Juan Antonio no conseguía pegar ojo por las noches. Cualquier ruidito lo despertaba: el murmullo de los árboles, los grillos, todo. Y por el día tanta paz y calma lo ponía nerviosísimo.

—¡Qué desastre!

B. *Conversación: Ventajas y desventajas.* You will hear a conversation, partially printed in your manual. Then you will participate in a similar conversaton. Complete it, based on your own experience. No answers will be given on the tape.

—¿Dónde estás más a gusto, en el campo o en la ciudad?

—Me encanta(n) _____ .

—¿Y qué te gusta hacer cuando estás allí?

—_____ .

—Pero también tiene sus inconvenientes, ¿no?

—¡ _____ !

UN POCO DE TODO

A. *Descripción: Una familia de la era de la tecnología.* You will hear five brief descriptions. Write the letter of each description next to the drawing that it describes. ¡OJO! Not all the drawings will be described. First, look at the drawings.

1.

2.

3.

4.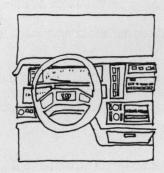

5.

6.

B. *Listening Passage.* You will hear an article from a Hispanic magazine about *Motorola de México.* It will be read twice. Then you will hear a series of statements about the article. Circle *C* if the statement is true or *F* if it is false. Answers to this exercise are given at the end of the tape.

1. C F   2. C F   3. C F   4. C F

C. *El sábado por la mañana.* Roberto and Laura have many things to do this morning. Listen carefully and number their activities from 1 to 5. First, listen to the list of things they have to do.

_____ llevar la impresora al taller

_____ ir al banco

_____ salir a cenar fuera

_____ pasar por la farmacia

_____ regresar a casa

CH. *Entrevista.* You will hear a series of questions. Answer, based on your own experience. No answer will be given on the tape.

1. ...   2. ...   3. ...   4. ...   5. ...   6. ...   7. ...   8. ...   9. ...

D. *Y para terminar... Una canción. La casita* is a *ranchera*, a type of Mexican ballad or folk song.

    La casita

¿Qué de dónde amigo vengo?	
De una casita que tengo	
más abajo del trigal;*	*más... below the wheat field*
de una casita chiquita,*	*muy pequeña*
para una mujer bonita	
que me quiera acompañar.	
Yedras* la tienen cubierta	*Ivy*
y un jazmín hay en la huerta*	*garden*
que las bardas ya cubrió;*	*que... that has already covered the fences*
en el portal* una hamaca,	*porch*
en el corral una vaca,*	*cow*
y adentro mi perro y yo.	
Más adentro está la cama	
muy olorosa a retama,*	*muy... smelling of broom*
limpiecita como usted;	
tengo también un armario,*	*closet*
un espejo* y un canario	*mirror*
que en la feria me merqué.*	*me... compré*
Si usted quiere la convido*	*invito*
a que visite ese nido*	*nest*
que hay abajo del trigal	
Le echo la silla* a Lucero,	*Le... I'll saddle up*
que nos llevará ligero*	*quickly*
hasta en medio del jacal.*	*house, hut*

Capítulo 15

PRIMERA PARTE

VOCABULARIO: PREPARACIÓN

A. *Definiciones:* You will hear a series of statements. Each will be said twice. Circle the letter of the word that is best defined by each.

1. a) la piscina   b) el traje de baño   4. a) la raqueta   b) la cancha

2. a) el golf   b) el fútbol   5. a) la red   b) el trofeo

3. a) el partido   b) el equipo

B. *Preguntas: Los ratos libres.* You will hear a series of questions about how you and others spent your free time in the past. Each will be said twice. Answer, using cues chosen from the following list. You will hear a possible answer on the tape. First, listen to the list.

     dar un paseo   esquiar
     hacer *camping*   nadar
     jugar a las cartas   tomar el sol

1. ...   2. ...   3. ...   4. ...   5. ...   6. ...

C. *¿Qué están haciendo estas personas?* When you hear the corresponding number, tell what the following people might be doing, using the present progressive. You will hear a possible answer on the tape.

1.

2.

3.

4.

CH. *Entrevista: Hablando de películas.* You will hear a series of questions. Each will be said twice. Answer, based on your own experience. You will hear a possible answer on the tape.

1. ...   2. ...   3. ...   4. ...

D. *Conversación: La vida de la gran ciudad.* You will hear a conversation, partially printed in your manual, about leisure-time activities in the city. Then you will participate in a similar conversation. Complete it, based on the cues suggested. You will hear a possible answer on the tape.

—¿Cómo pasas tus ratos libres aquí en la capital?

—A veces _____ .

—¿No te gusta visitar los museos de arte?

— _____ .

Here are the cues for your conversation:

caminar por el parque o pasear en bicicleta
no gustar / el arte, preferir / ir al teatro

PRONUNCIACIÓN Y ORTOGRAFÍA: *MORE ON STRESS AND THE WRITTEN ACCENT*

A. Repeat the following words, paying close attention to stress and the written accent.

1. bicicleta   cancha   trofeo   practican   estadios

2. ajedrez   jugador   tomar   legal   practicar

3. crédito   árbitro   vólibol   médico   máquina

4. corazón   natación   adiós   esquís   diversión

B. You have probably noticed that the written accent is an important factor in the spelling of some verb forms. It is also important for maintaining the original "sound" of a word to which syllables have been added.

When you hear the corresponding number, read the following pairs of words. Then repeat the correct pronunciation, imitating the speaker.

1. hablo / habló	5. gradúo / graduó	9. nación / naciones
2. pague / pagué	6. joven / jóvenes	10. francés / franceses
3. olvide / olvidé	7. diga / dígame	
4. limpio / limpió	8. haga / hágalo	

C. *Dictado.* You will hear the following words. Each will be said twice. Write in an accent mark, if necessary.

1. jugo	3. describes	5. sicologia
2. jugo	4. describemela	6. sicologo

7. almacen	9. levantate	11. gusto
8. almacenes	10. levanta	12. gusto

MINIDIÁLOGOS Y GRAMÁTICA

43. *Influencing Others: Tú Commands*

A. *Minidiálogo: En la escuela primaria: Frases útiles para la maestra.* You will hear a dialogue followed by a series of statements. Circle the letter of the person who might have made each statement.

1. a) una alumna   b) la maestra   3. a) una alumna   b) la maestra

2. a) una alumna   b) la maestra   4. a) una alumna   b) la maestra

B. *Un viaje en el coche de Raúl.* Form new sentences, using the oral cues.

1. —Raúl maneja muy mal. ¿Qué le pide Ud.? (no arrancar rápidamente) →
   —Raúl, <u>no arranques rápidamente</u>.

   a. ...   b. ...   c. ...

2. —Cuando el coche no funciona, ¿qué le dice Ud. a Raúl? (revisar el motor) →
   —<u>Revisa el motor</u>, Raúl.

   a. ...   b. ...   c. ...

C. *En el consultorio del médico.* Imagining that you are a doctor, tell your young patient Pepito what to do, using the oral cues and informal commands.

MODELO: (quitarse la camisa) → <u>Quítate la camisa, Pepito</u>.

1. ...   2. ...   3. ...   4. ...

CH. *Consejos.* Your friend Estela is about to do the following things. Advise her what to do or *not* do, using informal commands based on verbs from the following list. Add any other necessary information. You will hear a possible answer on the tape. First, listen to the list.

(no) comer tanto(a) _____   (no) tomar _____ (<u>curso</u>)

(no) llevar _____ al taller   (no) quejarse con _____

MODELO: (Me faltan dos cursos de idiomas para graduarme y no sé cuáles tomar.) →
Pues, toma el francés tres y una clase de conversación.

1. ... 2. ... 3. ... 4. ...

44. ¿Hay alguien que... ? ¿Hay un lugar donde... ? Subjunctive After Nonexistent and Indefinite Antecedents

A. En la plaza central. You will hear a series of statements about the drawing. Circle C if the statement is true or F if it is false.

1. C F

2. C F

3. C F

4. C F

B. ¿Sabe Ud. patinar? You will hear a series of sentences. Each will be said twice. Circle the appropriate letters to indicate whether the sentence refers to a known or to an as yet unknown person.

1. a) known   b) unknown   3. a) known   b) unknown

2. a) known   b) unknown   4. a) known   b) unknown

C. En busca de una casa nueva. Form new sentences, using the oral cues.

1. —¿Qué tipo de casa buscan Uds.? (estar en el campo) →
   —Buscamos una casa que esté en el campo.

   a. ... b. ... c. ... ch. ...

2. —¿Y cómo quieren Uds. que sean los vecinos? (jugar a las cartas) →
   —Queremos vecinos que jueguen a las cartas.

   a. ... b. ... c. ... ch. ...

SEGUNDA PARTE

CH. Escenas de la vida. You will hear a series of statements. Each will be said twice. Respond to each statement, using the written cues.

MODELO: (Necesitamos un abogado que hable español.) Pues, yo conozco... →
Pues, yo conozco un abogado que habla español.

1. Yo te puedo recomendar...

4. Pues yo también quiero tener...

2. Lo siento, pero no hay nadie aquí...

5. Ellos van a ofrecerte un puesto...

3. Pues yo busco...

D. *¿Qué tienen estas personas? ¿Y qué desean?* Tell what these people have and what they want, using the written cues. You will hear a possible answer on the tape.

MODELO:

viejo / nuevo →
Arturo tiene un auto (que es) viejo; desea uno
que sea nuevo.

1.

no tener vista / tener vista

2.

perezoso / trabajador

3.

grande / pequeño

4.

hacer mucho ruido / ser más tranquilos

45. *Expressing Contingency and Purpose: The Subjunctive After Certain Conjunctions*

A. *Minidiálogo: Unos verdaderos aficionados.* You will hear a dialogue followed by a series of statements. Circle *C* if the statement is true or *F* if it is false.

1. C   F

2. C   F

3. C   F

4. C   F

B. *Un viaje.* You will hear the following pairs of sentences. Then you will hear a conjunction. Join each pair of sentences, using the conjunction and making any necessary changes.

MODELO: (Hacemos el viaje. No cuesta mucho.) →
               <u>Hacemos el viaje con tal que no cueste mucho.</u>

1. Tenemos que salir. Empieza a llover.

2. No queremos ir. Hace sol.

3. Pon las maletas en el coche. Podemos salir pronto.

4. Trae el mapa. Nos perdemos.

Now answer the questions you hear, based on your interpretation of the preceding sentences. Each will be said twice. You will hear a possible answer on the tape.

1. ...   2. ...   3. ...   4. ...

C. *Descripción.* Circle the letter of the picture best described by the sentences you hear. Each sentence will be said twice.

1. a)   b)

2. a)    b)

3. a)    b)

4. a)    b)

CH. *¿Quién lo dijo?* When you hear the number, read each of the following statements, giving the present subjunctive form of the verbs in parentheses. You will hear the correct answer on the tape. Then you will hear the names of two different people. Circle the letter of the person who might have made each statement.

1. a   b   No les doy los paquetes a los clientes antes de que me (*pagar*).

2. a   b   Voy a revisar las llantas en caso de que (*necesitar*) aire.

3. a   b   No compro esa computadora a menos que (*ser*) fácil de manejar.

4. a   b   Voy a tomarle la temperatura al paciente antes de que lo (*ver*) la doctora.

SITUACIONES

A. *¿Qué quieres hacer?* You will hear two conversations about activities. Read them silently, along with the speakers.

Un fin de semana en la ciudad

—¿Qué hacen Uds. los fines de semana?

—Nos encanta pasear por la mañana, cuando hay poco tráfico.

—Sí, y a veces visitamos alguna exposición de arte y después tomamos el aperitivo en un café.

—¿Me invitan a ir con Uds. alguna vez?

—¡Encantados!

Delante del cine

—¡Hola, hombre! ¿Tú también vienes a ver *El museo de Drácula?*

—¡Qué va! Voy a ver *El Sol de Acapulco.*

—¿Por qué no nos acompañas? Está con nosotros Marisa, la prima de Carlos.

—Lo siento, pero voy a encontrarme con Elena Ortega... y además a mí me parecen pesadísimas las películas de horror.

—Hasta luego, entonces. Que lo pases bien.

—Chau. ¡Y que se diviertan!

B. Now you will participate in a similar conversation, partially printed in your manual, about a summer afternoon activity. Complete it, based on the cues suggested. No answers will be given on the tape.

—Hace mucho tiempo que no _____ .

—Pues, si quieres, puedes usar _____ .

—¿Qué te parece si vamos hasta el lago (*lake*)?

—¡Estupendo!... y podemos _____ .

Here are the cues for your conversation.

    la de mi amigo
    llevar unos sándwiches y algo para beber

UN POCO DE TODO

A. *Dictado: El viernes por la noche.* You will hear a brief theater ad, followed by a brief conversation. Each will be read twice. Listen carefully and write the requested information. First, listen to the list of information.

cuándo tiene lugar la función _____

el nombre de la comedia _____

la actriz principal _____

el nombre del teatro _____

el nombre de las personas que van a la función _____,

_____ y _____

B. *Conversación: De vacaciones.* You will hear a conversation, partially printed in your manual, about vacation plans. Then you will participate in a similar conversation. Complete it, based on the cues suggested.

—El mes que viene _____ .

—¿Cuánto tiempo piensan pasar allí?

— _____ . Vamos a _____ .

—Eso es lo que más les gusta a los niños, ¿verdad?

—Sí. _____ .

—Pues, ¡que se diviertan todos!

Here are the cues for your conversation.

> ir a la ciudad
> dos semanas / ir al teatro / visitar el museo de arte
> encantarnos las comedias y los cuadros (*paintings*) de Goya

C. *Listening Passage.* You will hear a brief passage about the movie industry in Hispanic countries. It will be read twice. Then you will hear a series of statements about the passage. Circle *C* if the statement is true or *F* if it is false. Answers to this exercise are given at the end of the tape.

The following word appears in the passage: *premio* (prize).

1. C F   2. C F   3. C F   4. C F   5. C F

CH. *Entrevista: Hablando de diversiones.* You will hear a series of questions. Each will be said twice. Answer, based on your own experience. No answers will be given on the tape.

1. ...   2. ...   3. ...   4. ...   5. ...   6. ...

D. *Y para terminar... Una canción.* The song *Cielito lindo* is popular throughout Hispanic America, and it is well known in some parts of the United States.

Cielito lindo

De la Sierra Morena,
Cielito lindo,* vienen bajando,   bonito
Un par de ojitos negros,
Cielito lindo,
De contrabando.

Coro

Ay, ay, ay, ay,
Canta y no llores,
Porque cantando se alegran,
Cielito lindo,
Los corazones. (*bis*)

Repaso 5

A. *Definiciones.* You will hear a series of definitions. Each will be said twice. Write the number of the definition next to the word that is best defined by each. First, listen to the list of words.

_____ el ciclismo   _____ la taquilla

_____ el ordenador   _____ la conductora

_____ la natación   _____ la programadora

_____ doblada   _____ el vólibol

B. *¿Dónde están estas personas?* You will hear a series of brief conversations or parts of conversations. Write the number of each next to the location in which the conversation might be taking place. First, listen to the list of locations.

_____ un estadio   _____ una cancha

_____ una gasolinera   _____ una tienda de computadoras

_____ un museo   _____ un teatro

C. *Conversación: Haciendo planes.* You will hear a conversation, partially printed in your manual, about plans for an afternoon. Then you will participate in a similar conversation. Complete it, based on the cues suggested. No answers will be given on the tape.

—¡Qué _____ hace! ¿Qué te parece si _____?

—No, gracias. Prefiero quedarme en casa. _____

está puesto y la temperatura es perfecta aquí adentro.

—Como quieras (*As you wish*)... _____ , pues.

—¡Que te diviertas!

Here are the cues for your conversation:

        frío / ir al Café Rioja a tomar un café
        ir (yo) sin ti

CH. *Dictado: El día del partido.* You will hear three brief phone conversations, all about the same soccer game. You will hear each one only once. Listen carefully and write the requested information. First, listen to the list of information.

el nombre de los equipos que van a jugar _____

el nombre de las personas que van al partido _____

lo que no le gusta a Héctor _____

la hora que empieza el partido _____

lo que van a hacer Héctor y su amiga _____

D. *Descripción*. Using the written cues, tell what the following people are doing when you hear their names. Use additional words to complete the meaning of each sentence. You will hear a possible answer on the tape.

MODELO:

 llenar

(el mecánico) → <u>El mecánico está llenando las llantas de aire.</u>

1.  estacionar

2.  editar

3.  patinar

4.  arreglar

5.  hacer *camping*

E. *Direcciones*. Your American friend Carla, who lives in another town, is visiting you. Today she plans to do some exploring of the city on her own. Using the map and words from the list, tell her how to get to the places she wants to visit. You will hear each of her questions twice, and you will hear a possible answer on the tape. First, listen to the list.

doblar	a la derecha
seguir todo derecho	a la izquierda
esquina	

Now look at the map, noting that your location is indicated with an arrow. The destinations Carla will ask about will be said now. You may want to circle them on the map.

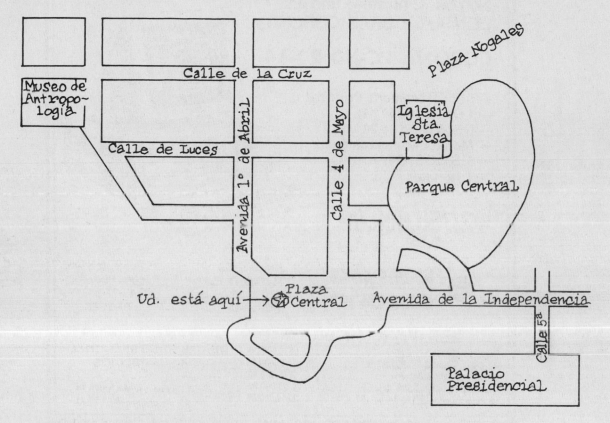

MODELO: Dime, ¿cómo puedo llegar a la Iglesia de Santa Teresa? →
            <u>Sigue todo derecho por la Calle Cuatro de Mayo y dobla a la derecha en</u>
            <u>la segunda esquina.</u>

1. ...   2. ...   3. ...

F. *En el periódico*. The following ad appeared in a Mexican newspaper. When you hear the corresponding number, give the Spanish equivalent of the words listed. First, take time to look at the ad.

1. hard disc

2. monochrome

3. tutorials

4. regulator

5. ...   6. ...   7. ...

G. *Entrevista: Temas diversos*. You will hear a series of questions. Each will be said twice. Answer, based on your own experience. No answers will be given on the tape.

1. ...   2. ...   3. ...   4. ...   5. ...   6. ...   7. ...   8. ...

Capítulo 16

PRIMERA PARTE

VOCABULARIO: PREPARACIÓN

A. *El noticiero del Canal Diez.* You will hear a brief "newsbreak" from a television station. Then you will hear a series of statements about the newscast. Circle *C* if the statement is true or *F* if it is false.

1. C F   2. C F   3. C F   4. C F

B. *Definiciones.* You will hear a series of statements. Each will be said twice. Place the number of the statement next to the word that is best defined by each. First, listen to the list of words.

_____ una guerra   _____ la testigo

_____ la prensa   _____ el reportero

_____ un dictador   _____ la huelga

_____ los terroristas

C. *¿Qué creen Uds.?* You will hear a series of statements that describe the world today. React to each, using the written cues.

MODELO: (Hay tantas guerras en el mundo.) es lástima →
            Es lástima que haya tantas guerras en el mundo.

1. No dudo...   4. Es increíble...

2. No creemos...   5. No les gusta a los políticos...

3. Es probable...   6. Es verdad...

CH. *Entrevista.* You will hear a series of questions. Each will be said twice. Answer, based on your own experience. You will hear a possible answer on the tape.

1. ...   2. ...   3. ...   4. ...   5. ...   6. ...

D. *Dictado: Asociaciones.* You will hear several groups of words. Each group will be said twice. Write out the one word in each group that is *not* related and repeat it.

1. _____   3. _____

2. _____   4. _____

PRONUNCIACIÓN Y ORTOGRAFÍA: *MORE ON STRESS AND THE WRITTEN ACCENT*

A. You have probably noticed that when a pair of words is written the same but has different meanings, one of the words is accented. This accent is called a *diacritical* accent.

Repeat the following words, paying close attention to the meaning of each.

1. mi (*my*) / mí (*me*)

2. tu (*your*) / tú (*you*)

3. el (*the*) / él (*he*)

4. si (*if*) / sí (*yes*)

5. se (*oneself*) / sé (*I know; be* - informal command)

6. de (*of, from*) / dé (*give* - formal command; *give* - present subjunctive)

7. te (*you, yourself*) / té (*tea*)

8. solo (*alone, sole* - adjective) / sólo (*only* - adverb)

9. que (*that, which*) / ¿qué? (*what?*)

10. este (*this*) / éste (*this one*)

B. *Dictado.* Listen to the following sentences and determine by context whether or not the meaning of the underlined words requires a written accent. Each sentence will be said twice.

1. Creo que ese regalo es para mi.

2. Aquí esta tu te. ¿Que más quieres?

3. El dijo que te iba a llamar a las ocho.

4. Si, mi amigo se llama Antonio.

C. *Repaso:* Written accent. You will hear a series of words. Each will be said twice. Listen carefully and circle the letter of the word you hear.

1. a) tomas   b) Tomás   4. a) baile   b) bailé

2. a) gusto   b) gustó   5. a) interprete   b) intérprete

3. a) papa   b) papá   6. a) estudio   b) estudió

MINIDIÁLOGOS Y GRAMÁTICA

46. *¡Ojalá que pudiéramos hacerlo!:* Past Subjunctive

A. *Minidiálogo: Aquéllos eran otros tiempos...* You will hear a brief dialogue and commentary, followed by a series of statements. Circle *C* if the statement is true or *F* if it is false.

1. C F
2. C F
3. C F

VIEJOS VOTANTES.—¿Recuerda cuánto tuvimos que discurrir usted y yo antes de votar hace treinta años?

B. *Recuerdos.* Form new sentences, using the oral cues.

1. —Cuando Ud. estudiaba en la secundaria, ¿qué le gustaba? (estudiar idiomas) →
   —Me gustaba que <u>estudiáramos idiomas</u>.

   a. ...   b. ...   c. ...   ch. ...

2. —De niña, ¿cómo era su vida? (ser buena) →
   —Mis padres querían que <u>fuera buena</u>.

   a. ...   b. ...   c. ...   ch. ...

C. *¿Qué pasó ayer en el almacén?* You will hear the following statements from store employees. Using the oral cues, restate each to express a past event.

MODELO: No *quieren* que lo hagamos. (querían) → <u>No *querían* que lo hiciéramos.</u>

1. No *creo* que tengamos que trabajar tarde hoy.

2. Pero el jefe *insiste* en que nos quedemos hasta las ocho.

3. *Es* necesario que hagamos el inventario.

4. No *hay* nadie que esté contento con estas condiciones de trabajo.

5. Le *decimos* al jefe que *vamos* a hacer una huelga a menos que nos dé un aumento.

CH. *¿Qué quería Ud.?* You are never happy with your family's plans. What would you have rather done? Use the written cues to tell what you preferred, beginning with *Yo quería que...*

MODELO: (Ayer cenamos en el restaurante El Perico Negro.) casa →
            <u>Yo quería que cenáramos en casa.</u>

1. comedia   4. computadora

2. campo   5. arroz

3. dar un paseo

D. *El noticiero del mediodía: Un informe especial.* You will hear a radio newscast. It will be read twice. Then you will hear a series of statements about the newscast. Circle *C* if the statement is true or *F* if it is false.

1. C F   2. C F   3. C F   4. C F

E. *Entrevista: Hablando del pasado.* You will hear a series of questions. Each will be said twice. Answer, based on your own experience. You will hear a possible answer on the tape.

1. ...   2. ...   3. ...   4. ...   5. ...   6. ...

SEGUNDA PARTE

47. *More About Expressing Possession: Stressed Possessives*

A. *Minidiálogo: En el hotel.* You will hear dialogue followed by three statements. Circle the number of the statement that best summarizes the dialogue.

1   2   3

B. *¿A qué se refiere?* You will hear a series of sentences containing stressed possessive pronouns. Circle the letter of the word to which the pronoun in each sentence might refer.

1. a) la cuenta   b) las cuentas   4. a) los zapatos   b) las corbatas

2. a) los papeles   b) las cartas   5. a) los abrigos   b) el ordenador

3. a) el asiento   b) la ropa

C. *Hablando de lo que nos pertenece* (belongs). Form new sentences, using the oral cues.

—La <u>computadora</u> de Antonio está rota. ¿Y la tuya? →
—¿La <u>mía</u>? Ya <u>la</u> he arreglado.

1. ...   2. ...   3. ...   4. ...

CH. *Entrevista: Comparaciones.* A friend from another university is describing his home and school environments. He then asks how they compare to your own. Each description will be said twice. Answer his questions according to the model. You will hear a possible answer on the tape.

MODELO: (Hay 65.000 estudiantes en mi universidad. ¿Cuál es más grande, mi universidad o la tuya?) → <u>La tuya es más grande que la mía.</u>

1. ...   2. ...   3. ...   4. ...

SITUACIONES

A. *Hablando de las noticias.* You will hear two dialogues about world events. Read the dialogues silently, along with the speakers.

En la televisión

—¿Oíste lo del último accidente de aviación?

—¿Te refieres al accidente en que murieron cerca de 150 personas?

—Sí. Dicen que sucedió por pura negligencia.

—Es difícil creerlo, ¿no? Parece imposible que el piloto no pudiera hacer nada para evitarlo.

—Bueno, hay que tomar en cuenta que es posible que el avión tuviera un desperfecto.

—No creo que fuera eso... Si las autoridades se interesaran más por proteger al público...

—Bueno. Es cuestión de opiniones. Personalmente creo que sí se interesan.

—¡Pero no lo suficiente! Yo creo que...

En el periódico

—¿Algo nuevo?

—¡Qué va! Centroamérica está a punto de estallar, la tensión sigue creciendo en el Golfo Pérsico, la situación en el Oriente Medio continúa igual de catastrófica...

—Ya veo. Lo de siempre.

B. Now you will participate in a conversation, partially printed in your manual, about the latest news. Complete it, based on the cues suggested. You will hear a possible answer on the tape.

—¿Has oído _____?

—No. ¿Qué pasó? Nada malo, espero.

—Pues, _____ .

— _____

Here are the cues for your conversation.

      el noticiero del Canal Ocho
      explotar otra bomba terrorista en Europa / haber muchos heridos (*wounded people*)

UN POCO DE TODO

A. *Dictado: Hablando de las elecciones.* You will hear a brief conversation between Alberto and Raquel. It will be read twice. Listen carefully and jot down the requested information in the spaces provided. First, listen to the list of requested information.

el nombre de la candidata que perdió las elecciones _____

el nombre del candidato que ganó las elecciones _____

el porcentaje (*percentage*) de los ciudadanos que votó por la candidata que perdió _____

la cuestión principal de la campaña _____

B. *Listening Passage.* You will hear a brief passage about one aspect of the economic system of Latin America, *el pluriempleo.* It will be read twice. Then you will hear a series of questions about the passage. Choose the best answer to each. Answers to this exercise are given at the end of the tape.

1. a) Es tener más de un empleo.

   b) Es trabajar por la noche.

2. a) Tendría que ser rico o ser un profesor eminente.

   b) Podría vivir bien sólo con el sueldo de profesor.

3. a) Predomina en la clase alta.

   b) Predomina en la clase baja y en la clase media.

4. a) Sí, corresponde al estereotipo del latino perezoso.

   b) No, no corresponde al estereotipo del latino perezoso.

C. *Dictado: Unas vacaciones inolvidables* (unforgettable). You will hear the following paragraph, partially printed below. It will be read twice. Listen carefully and supply the missing words.

La última vez que _____ ^{1} al campo para las vacaciones, todo _____ ^{2}

desastroso. _____ ^{3} a _____ ^{4} dos semanas idílicas en las montañas, en una

casita que pertenece (*belongs*) a mi tío. Pero antes de que _____ ^{5} de la ciudad, nos

_____ ^{6} cuenta de que _____ ^{7} una llanta desinflada. Por fin _____ ^{8}

la llanta y nos _____ ^{9} en marcha, pero a mitad de camino _____ ^{10} que se nos

_____ ^{11} _____ ^{12} el mapa y nos _____ ^{13}. _____ ^{14}

dos horas _____ ^{15} por caminos rurales. Yo _____ ^{16} que _____ ^{17}

a la ciudad, pero mi padre _____ ^{18} en que _____ ^{19} _____ ^{20} la

casita de mi tío. Bueno, la _____ ^{21} por fin, a la una de la mañana. Al día siguiente,

_____ ^{22} a llover y no _____ ^{23} de _____ ^{24} hasta el día en que

_____25 a casa. Para las próximas vacaciones, ¡_____26 _____27

en casa!

Now you will hear a series of statements about the preceding paragraph. Each will be said twice. Circle *C* if the statement is true or *F* if it is false.

1.　C　F　　2.　C　F　　3.　C　F　　4.　C　F　　5.　F　C

CH. *Descripción: Escenas actuales.* You will hear the following cartoon captions. Then you will hear a series of questions. Each will be said twice. Answer, based on the cartoons and your own experience.

—Lo bueno de las campañas políticas es que no te las pueden repetir.

1. ...　　2. ...　　3. ...　　4. ...

—No veáis mucha televisión... Dentro de tres crímenes y seis asaltos apagáis el aparato.

5. ...   6. ...   7. ...   8. ...

D. *Entrevista.* You will hear a series of questions. Each will be said twice. Answer, based on your own experience. No answers will be given on the tape.

1. ...   2. ...   3. ...   4. ...   5. ...

E. *Y para terminar... Una canción. Adelita* is a traditional Mexican song that originated during the Mexican Revolution.

Adelita

Si Adelita se fuera con otro,
La seguiría por tierra y por mar,
Si por mar en un buque* de guerra,   *boat*
Y por tierra en un tren militar.

Y si acaso yo muero en la guerra,
Y mi cuerpo en la tierra va a quedar,
Adelita, por Dios, te lo ruego
Que por mí no vayas a llorar.

Capítulo 17

PRIMERA PARTE

VOCABULARIO: PREPARACIÓN

A. *Dictado: Asociaciones.* You will hear several groups of words. Each group will be said twice. Write out the one word in each group that is not related and repeat it.

1. _____   3. _____

2. _____   4. _____

B. *Asuntos financieros.* You will hear a series of situations. Each will be described twice. Choose the most logical response to each situation.

1. a) Dejo de comprar cosas innecesarias.   b) Gasto más en diversiones.

2. a) Busco un compañero para compartir   b) Me mudo a un apartamento más caro.
   (*share*) el alquiler.

3. a) Me quejo con el departamento de   b) Pago los $20,00.
   créditos.

4. a) Pago al contado.   b) Pago con cheque.

5. a) Pago al contado.   b) Pago a plazos.

C. You will hear a brief conversation between two friends, Beatriz and Magali, followed by a series of statements. Circle *C* if the statement is true or *F* if it is false.

1. C F   2. C F   3. C F   4. C F

CH. *Descripción.* You will hear a series of questions. Each will be said twice. Answer, based on the drawing. You will hear a possible answer on the tape.

1. ...

2. ...

3. ...

4. ...

5. ...

D. *En el periódico.* You will hear a brief ad for *el Grupo Banco Exterior de España.* Then you will hear two statements. Circle the number of the statement that best summarizes the ad.

1   2

PORTUGAL
BANCO EXTERIOR DE ESPAÑA
Oficina de Representación

GRUPO BANCO EXTERIOR
El banco sin fronteras

Para trabajar en una Europa sin fronteras, usted necesita un banco sin fronteras.

El Banco Exterior de España es un experto en comercio internacional con todo el mundo y especialmente con la Europa Comunitaria.

Por eso, el Exterior tiene desde hace años una amplia red de bancos, sucursales y oficinas de representación en los países del Mercado Común.

Esta red y su experiencia en comercio exterior permiten al Grupo ofrecerle los conocimientos profesionales y la cobertura geográfica para hacer más fáciles y rápidas todas sus transacciones personales, profesionales y empresariales con los países de la CEE.

Olvide las fronteras, aproveche la conexión.

E. *Conversación: Entre amigos.* You will hear a conversation, partially printed in your manual, about a loan. Then you will participate in a similar conversation about another kind of loan. Complete it, based on the cues suggested. You will hear a possible answer on the tape.

—Oye, ¿_____ ?

—¡Hombre! Bueno... si me los devuelves lo antes posible.

—Cómo no. _____ a más tardar (*at the latest*).

—¿Para qué necesitas tanto dinero?

— _____ .

Here are the cues for your conversation:

    coche viejo
    el lunes próximo
    el mío / estar en el taller

PRONUNCIACIÓN Y ORTOGRAFÍA: *COGNATE PRACTICE*

A. Repeat the following words, paying close attention to the differences in spelling between the word and its English cognate.

1.	correcto	5.	teléfono	9.	alianza
2.	teoría	6.	anual	10.	físico
3.	arcángel	7.	clasificar	11.	patético
4.	químico	8.	afirmar	12.	ateísmo

B. *Dictado.* You will hear the following words. Each will be said twice. Listen carefully and write the missing letters.

1. _____ os _____ ato   5. o _____ osición

2. a _____ ención   6. _____ otogra _____ ía

3. a _____ oníaco   7. co _____ e _____ ión

4. _____ cología   8. ar _____ itecto

MINIDIÁLOGOS Y GRAMÁTICA

48. *Talking About the Future: Future Verb Forms*

A. *Minidiálogo: ¡Hay que reducir los gastos! ¿Qué vamos a hacer?*
You will hear a dialogue followed by a series of statements from the dialogue. Tell whether each statement would add to or reduce the family's expenses.

1. a) aumentar   b) reducir

2. a) aumentar   b) reducir

3. a) aumentar   b) reducir

4. a) aumentar   b) reducir

B. *Dictado: ¿Pretérito o futuro?* You will hear a series of sentences. Each will be said twice. Listen carefully and write the verbs you hear in the appropriate column.

Pretérito	Futuro
_____	_____
_____	_____
_____	_____

C. *El viernes por la tarde.* Using the oral and written cues, tell what the following people will do with their paychecks.

1. Bernardo

2. algunos empleados

3. Adela y yo

4. tú... ¿verdad?

5. yo

CH. *El cumpleaños de Jaime.* Jaime's birthday is next week. Answer the questions about his birthday, using the written cues.

MODELO: (¿Cuántos años va a cumplir Jaime?) dieciocho → <u>Cumplirá dieciocho años</u>.

1. sus amigos y sus parientes

2. una videograbadora

3. un pastel de chocolate

4. discos

5. feliz cumpleaños

D. *Conjeturas.* You will hear a series of sentences. Restate each to express probability or conjecture.

MODELO: (¿Dónde vive?) → <u>¿Dónde vivirá?</u>

El nuevo empleado en la oficina:

1. ...   2. ...   3. ...

La visita de la tía Ernestina:

4. ...   5. ...   6. ...

E. *Entrevista: Hablando del futuro.* You will hear a series of questions. Each will be said twice. Answer, based on your own experience. You will hear a possible answer on the tape.

1. ...   2. ...   3. ...   4. ...   5. ...

49. *Expressing Future or Pending Actions: Subjunctive and Indicative After Conjunctions of Time*

A. *Mafalda.* You will hear the caption for the following cartoon. Then you will hear a series of statements. Circle the letter of the person who might have made each statement.

1. a) Mafalda   b) el padre de Mafalda

2. a) Mafalda   b) el padre de Mafalda

3. a) Mafalda   b) el padre de Mafalda

SEGUNDA PARTE

B. *Dictado.* You will hear the following sentences. Each will be said twice. Write the missing words.

1. Voy a darte el dinero en cuanto _____ el cheque.

2. Nos llamarán tan pronto como _____ .

3. Siempre comemos en un restaurante elegante cuando mis tíos nos _____ .

4. Anoche bailamos hasta que la orquesta _____ de tocar.

C. *Escenas de la vida cotidiana.* You will hear the following pairs of sentences. Combine them to form one complete sentence, using the oral cues.

MODELO: Voy a decidirlo. Hablo con él. (después de que) →
               <u>Voy a decidirlo después de que hable con él.</u>

1. Elisa se va a despertar. Oye el despertador.

2. No voy a estar contenta. Recibo un aumento.

3. Iba a mudarme a un apartamento. Mis padres vendieron su casa.

4. Comimos. Llegaron los niños. (¡OJO!)

5. Tito, apaga la luz. Has terminado.

6. Querían que les mandara una tarjeta postal. Yo salí del Perú.

CH. *Antes del viaje*. You will hear a series of questions. Answer in the negative, using the written cues.

MODELO: (¿Ya hiciste las reservaciones?) llamar al agente de viajes →
<u>No, las haré cuando llame al agente de viajes</u>.

1. cobrar el cheque semanal
2. darme tu ropa
3. ir al centro
4. tener tiempo
5. ir al consulado

D. *Descripción*. Tell what is happening in the following drawings by answering the questions. You will hear a possible answer on the tape.

MODELO: (¿Hasta cuándo va a esperar Ricardo?) →
<u>Hasta que llegue Gerardo</u>.

1.

2.

3.

4.

SITUACIONES

A. *Cambiando dinero en un banco*. You will hear two dialogues about changing money in a foreign country. Read the dialogues silently, along with the speakers.

Al entrar

—Por favor. Quisiera cambiar moneda.

—Pase a la ventanilla 14, donde pone Cambio.

—Gracias, ¿eh?

—De nada.

Hablando con el cajero

—Sí, dígame. ¿Qué desea?

—Quisiera cambiar unos cheques de viajero en dólares a pesetas.

—¿Cuántos dólares quiere cambiar?

—Doscientos dólares, por favor. ¿A cuánto está el cambio hoy?

—A ciento veinte. ¿Ya firmó los cheques?

—Sí.

—Su pasaporte, por favor.

—Aquí lo tiene.

—Pase Ud. a la Caja con este recibo. La llamarán por este número.

—¿Y cuándo me devuelven el pasaporte?

—En la Caja, señorita.

B. Now you will participate in a similar conversation, partially printed in your manual, about exchanging a different amount of money. Complete the conversation, based on the cues suggested. You will hear a possible answer on the tape. ¡OJO! The cues are not in sequence.

—¿En qué puedo servirle?

—_____ .

—¿Cuántos dólares desea cambiar?

—_____ . ¿ _____ ?

—A ciento sesenta y uno. ¿Ya firmó los cheques?

—_____ .

—Déme su pasaporte, por favor, y pase a la Caja con este recibo. Allí lo llamarán por este número; le

devolverán su pasaporte y le darán el dinero.

—_____ .

Here are the cues for your conversation:

> querer cambiar estos cheques de viajero a pesetas
> gracias
> sí, aquí tenerlos (Ud.)
> mil dólares / ¿a cuánto estar el cambio?

UN POCO DE TODO

A. *Situaciones: ¿Qué cree Ud. que van a hacer estas personas?* You will hear three situations. Each will be said twice. Choose the most logical solution for each and repeat it.

1. a) Teresa comprará un coche barato y económico.

   b) Comprará un coche caro y lujoso.

   c) No comprará ningún coche.

2. a) Basilio tendrá que conseguir otro puesto para pagar el nuevo alquiler.

   b) Robará un banco.

   c) Compartirá (*He will share*) su apartamento con cuatro amigos.

3. a) Luisa empezará a poner el dinero que gasta en diversiones en su cuenta de ahorros.

   b) Les dirá a sus padres que no podrá comprarles un regalo este año.

   c) Insistirá en que su jefe le dé un aumento de sueldo inmediatamente.

B. *Listening Passage.* You will hear a brief passage about the *Banco Interamericano de Desarrollo* (*el BID*). It will be read twice. Then you will hear a series of statements about the passage. Circle *C* if the statement is true or *F* if it is false. Answers to this exercise are given at the end of the tape.

1. C F   2. C F   3. C F   4. C F

C. *Conversación: ¡La vida es cara!* You will hear a brief conversation between Sonia and David. Then you will hear a series of questions. Answer, based on the conversation and your own experience.

1. ...   2. ...   3. ...   4. ...   5. ...   6. ...

CH. *Descripción: Escenas actuales.* You will hear a series of questions. Each will be said twice. Answer, based on the following cartoons and your own experience. You will hear a possible answer on the tape. First, listen to the cartoon captions.

1. ...   2. ...   3. ...

4. ...   5. ...   6. ...   7. ...

D. *Y para terminar... Una canción.* The song *Las mañanitas* is a traditional song that is sung—very early in the morning—to a woman on her birthday.

Las mañanitas

Éstas son las mañanitas
Que cantaba el Rey* David   *King*
A las muchachas bonitas.
Se las cantaba así:

Despierta, mi bien,* despierta, mi... *my dear*
Mira que ya amaneció.*   *it has dawned*
Ya los pajarillos* cantan,   *little birds*
La luna ya se metió.*   se... *disappeared*

Qué linda* está la mañana   bonita
En que vengo a saludarte.* *to greet you*
Venimos todos con gusto*   con... *gladly*
Y placer a felicitarte.

Con jazmines y flores
Te venimos a cantar.
Levántate de mañana.
Mira, que ya amaneció.

Capítulo 18

PRIMERA PARTE

VOCABULARIO: PREPARACIÓN

A. *¿A quién necesitan en estas situaciones?* You will hear a series of situations. Circle the letter of the person or professional who would best be able to help. Do not be distracted by unfamiliar vocabulary; concentrate instead on the main idea of each situation.

1. a) un arquitecto   b) un carpintero

2. a) una dentista   b) una enfermera

3. a) una consejera matrimonial   b) un policía

4. a) una fotógrafa   b) un bibliotecario

5. a) un plomero   b) una electricista

B. *¿Quiénes son?* Using the list of professions below, identify these people after you hear the corresponding number. Begin each sentence with *Es un...* or *Es una...* First, listen to the list of professions.

obrero/a	cocinero/a
peluquero/a	fotógrafo/a
periodista	plomero/a
veterinario/a	hombre o mujer de negocios

C. *En busca de un puesto.* You are looking for a new job in a large corporation. Tell how you will go about getting the job, using phrases from the following list. First, listen to the list, then put the remaining items in order, from 3 to 6. Then, when you hear the number, tell what you will do.

_____ tratar de caerle bien al entrevistador

_____ aceptar el puesto y renunciar a mi puesto actual (*present*)

_2_ pedirle una solicitud de empleo

____ ir a la entrevista

____ llenar la solicitud a máquina

_1_ llamar a la directora de personal

MODELO: 1. llamar a la directora de personal → <u>Llamo a la directora de personal</u>.

2. ...   3. ...   4. ...   5. ...   6. ...

CH. *Dictado: Quejas de la oficina.* You overhear a series of statements coming from a closed-door meeting between management and employees. You will hear each statement twice. Listen carefully and write down the complaints in the appropriate blank.

Las quejas de los empleados:

1. _____

2. _____

3. _____

Las quejas de los jefes:

4. _____

5. _____

6. _____

D. *En el periódico: Empleos.* You will hear three job ads from Hispanic newspapers. Each will be read twice. Write the number of the ad next to the name of the person who might want the job. First, listen to the list of candidates.

____ Ricardo es carpintero. Siempre le ha gustado hacer cosas de madera. El año pasado le hizo un estante muy bonito a su madre. También ha hecho otros muebles.

____ Sabrina sabe hablar español, inglés y alemán. También sabe escribir a máquina y usar una computadora. Es una persona muy eficiente y organizada.

____ Julia ha trabajado en la industria petrolera por ocho años. Es ingeniera, pero también ha tenido a su cargo la planeación de proyectos y el análisis de su costo.

PRONUNCIACIÓN Y ORTOGRAFÍA: *MORE COGNATE PRACTICE*

A. *False Cognates.* Unlike true cognates, false cognates do not have the same meaning in English as they do in Spanish. Repeat the following words, some of which you have already seen and used actively, paying close attention to their pronunciation and true meaning in Spanish.

la carta (*letter*)   el éxito (*success*)   embarazada (*pregnant*)
dime (*tell me*)   sin (*without*)   el pariente (*relative*)
emocionante (*thrilling*)   el pie (*foot*)   dice (*he/she says*)
asistir (*to attend*)   actual (*current, present-day*)   la red (*net*)
el pan (*bread*)   actualmente (*nowadays*)

B. You will hear the following paragraph from an article in a Spanish newspaper. Pay close attention to the pronunciation of the indicated cognates. Then you will practice reading the paragraph. You may want to record your reading.

El *ministro* de *Transportes* y *Comunicaciones*, Abel Caballero, ha *declarado* que el Gobierno está dando los primeros pasos para la *construcción* de un *satélite* español de *telecomunicaciones* que, de tomarse la *decisión final*, *comenzará* a ser *operativo* en 1992. (...)

Muchos de los *componentes* del *satélite* tendrían que ser *importados*, pero al menos el treinta y seis por ciento los podría construir la *industria* española.

MINIDIÁLOGOS Y GRAMÁTICA

50. Expressing What You Would Do: Conditional Verb Forms

A. *Minidiálogo: La fantasía de una maestra de primaria.* You will hear a teacher's description of how she would like her life to be. Then you will hear three statements. Circle the letter of the statement that best summarizes the teacher's description.

1

2

3

B. *¿Imperfecto o condicional?* You will hear a series of sentences. Each will be said twice. Circle the letter of the verb contained in each, imperfect or conditional.

1. a) imperfecto   b) condicional   4. a) imperfecto   b) condicional

2. a) imperfecto   b) condicional   5. a) imperfecto   b) condicional

3. a) imperfecto   b) condicional

C. *¿Qué harían para mejorar las condiciones?* Using the oral and written cues, tell what the following people would like to do to improve the world.

MODELO: (Betty) eliminar las guerras → <u>Betty eliminaría las guerras</u>.

1. desarrollar otros tipos de energía   4. eliminar el hambre y las desigualdades

2. construir viviendas para todos   5. protestar por el uso de las armas atómicas

3. eliminar a los terroristas   6. matar a los dictadores

CH. *Entrevista.* You will hear a series of questions. Each will be said twice. Answer, based on your own experience. No answers will be given on the tape.

1. ... 2. ... 3. ... 4. ... 5. ...

51. Expressing Hypothetical Situations: What if . . . ?: Conditional Sentences

A. *Minidiálogo: Una entrevista en la dirección del Canal 45.* You will hear a dialogue followed by a series of statements. Circle *C* if the statement is true or *F* if it is false.

1. C F
2. C F
3. C F

SEGUNDA PARTE

B. *Situaciones.* You will hear three brief situations. Circle the letter of the best reaction to each.

1. a) ...regresaría a casa en autobús   b) ...llamaría a la policía inmediatamente

2. a) ...escribiría un cheque   b) ...me ofrecería a lavar los platos

3. a) ...trataría de negociar con el líder del sindicato laboral   b) ...despediría a todos los empleados

C. *Consejos.* Your friend Pablo has a problem with his roommates. What would you do in his place? Answer, using the oral cues.

MODELO: (llamar a mis padres) → <u>Si yo fuera Pablo, llamaría a mis padres.</u>

1. ... 2. ... 3. ... 4. ...

CH. *Durante la campaña.* Your friend Nicanor makes the following statements. Contradict what he says, according to the model.

MODEL: Aquel senador no es conservador. → <u>Sí, pero habla como si fuera conservador.</u>

1. El candidato Molina no cree en los derechos humanos.

2. El gobernador no protege el medio ambiente.

3. Al gobernador no le interesan los problemas de los inmigrantes.

4. Ese candidato no toma en cuenta la opinión de las mujeres.

D. *Las finanzas*. You will hear the following sentences. Restate each, using the conditional.

MODELO: No le ofrecerán el puesto a menos que tenga buenas recomendaciones. →
            <u>Le ofrecerían el puesto si tuviera buenas recomendaciones</u>.

1. No le harán el préstamo a menos que esté trabajando.

2. No ahorraré más dinero a menos que controle mis gastos.

3. No pagaré las cuentas antes de que reciba el cheque semanal.

4. No te cobrarán el cheque hasta que lo firmes.

SITUACIONES

A. *El mundo del trabajo*. You will hear two dialogues about jobs and careers. Read them silently, along with the speakers.

Hablando de la entrevista

—¿Qué tal te fue esta mañana?

—Pues no sé qué decirte. Me dijeron que me avisarían en una semana. ¿Y a ti?

—Lo mismo, pero no creo que me lo den. Tenían mucho interés en la experiencia que pudieran tener los candidatos, y como sabes, no tengo ninguna.

Hablando con los amigos

—¡Hola! ¿Ya tienes trabajo?

—¡Qué más quisiera! Me gustaría trabajar en lo mío, pero de momento no hay nada.

—Por lo visto los futuros biólogos no interesan demasiado...

—Hombre, a veces pienso que si volviera a entrar en la universidad, cambiaría de carrera, porque voy a tardar en colocarme de biólogo.

—Pues, no es sólo en lo tuyo. No sé si te acuerdas, pero yo tardé medio año en colocarme. ¡Y ahora llevo siete meses trabajando! O sea, ¡ánimo!

B. *Hablando con el entrevistador*. Now you will participate in an interview in which the director of personnel is interviewing you for a job in your area, *su campo*. Listen carefully; you will hear each question only once. Answer, based on your own experience. No answers will be given on the tape.

1. ...   2. ...   3. ...   4. ...   5. ...   6. ...

UN POCO DE TODO

A. *¡Entendiste mal!* Make statements about your plans, using the written cues when you hear the corresponding numbers. Make any necessary changes or additions. When your friend Alicia misunderstands your statements, correct her. Follow the model.

MODELO: llegar / trece / junio →
            UD.:   Llegaré el trece de junio.
       ALICIA: ¿No dijiste que llegarías el tres?
            UD.:   ¡No, no, no! Te dije que llegaría el trece. Entendiste mal.

1. estar / bar / doce

2. estudiar / Juan

3. ir / vacaciones / junio

4. verte / casa

5. tomar / tres / clases

B. *Listening Passage.* You will hear a brief passage about people who migrate in search of jobs. It will be read twice. Then you will hear a series of statements about the passage. Circle *C* if the statement is true or *F* if it is false. Answers to this exercise are given at the end of the tape.

1. C F   2. C F   3. C F   4. C F

C. *¿Qué haría Ud.?* Tell what you would do in these locations when you hear the corresponding number. You will hear a possible answer on the tape.

MODELO:

→ Si estuviera en la biblioteca, leería un libro.

1.

2.

3.

4.

5.

CH. *En el periódico: Empleos.* The following ads for jobs appeared in a Mexican newspaper. Choose the ad you are most interested in, based on the profession, and scan it. Answer the questions you hear, based on that ad. If the information requested is not in the ad, say *No lo dice*. No answers will be given on the tape. First, look at the ads.

1. ...   2. ...   3. ...   4. ...   5. ...

D. *Entrevista.* You will hear a series of questions. Each will be said twice. Answer, based on your own experience. You will hear a possible answer on the tape.

1. ...   2. ...   3. ...   4. ...

E. *Y para terminar... Una canción. De colores* is a song from the Chicano tradition in the United States.

De colores

De colores, de colores se visten los campos* en la primavera.	*fields*
De colores, de colores son los pajaritos que vienen de fuera.	
De colores, de colores es el arco iris* que vemos lucir.*	arco... *rainbow* *shine*
Y por eso los grandes amores de muchos colores me gustan a mí. (*bis*)	
Canta el gallo,* canta el gallo con el quiri, quiri, quiri, quiri, quiri.	*rooster*
La gallina,* la gallina con el cara, cara, cara, cara, cara.	*hen*
Los polluelos,* los polluelos con el pío, pío, pío, pío, pí.	*chicks*
Y por eso los grandes amores de muchos colores me gustan a mí. (*bis*)	

Repaso 6

A. *¿Dónde están?* You will hear four brief conversations or parts of conversations. Write the number of the conversation next to the place in which the speakers might be. First, listen to the list of locations.

_____ el consultorio de un médico   _____ el taller de una gasolinera

_____ un banco   _____ una tienda de computadoras

_____ la oficina de la directora de personal

B. *Hablando de ordenadores.* You will hear the following sentences. Form one complete sentence, using the oral cues. Follow the model.

MODELO: No compramos ese ordenador. Nos dan un buen precio. (a menos que) →
                 No compramos ese ordenador a menos que nos den un buen precio.

1. No compres esa impresora. Te enseñan a usarla.

2. Mándame uno de tus discos. Puedo copiarlo.

3. Voy a editar los textos. Compro un nuevo programa.

4. No salgas esta tarde. Llama la técnica.

C. *¿De quién son estas cosas?* You will hear a series of questions. Answer in the negative, using the written cues to complete your answer.

MODELO: (¿El libro es de Jacinta?) más viejo → No, no es suyo. El suyo es más viejo.

1. extranjero   4. para balcón

2. negros   5. de dos pisos y está en el campo

3. de lana

CH. *Todos tenemos derechos...* You will hear a brief conversation between Graciela and Miguel. It will be followed by a series of questions. Answer, based on the conversation and your own experience.

The following expression appears in the conversation: lo que me da la gana (*what I feel like*)

1. ...   2. ...   3. ...   4. ...   5. ...   6. ...

D. *Dictado: El noticiero del mediodía* (noon). You will hear a radio newscast. It will be read twice. Listen carefully and write down the requested information. First, listen to the list of information.

la fecha del noticiero _____

el tiempo que hace _____

el nombre de la fábrica donde terminó la huelga _____

lo qué decidió darles a los obreros el dueño de la fábrica _____

_____

la fecha en que regresan al trabajo los obreros _____

el mes en que se jugará el campeonato _____

la temperatura alta durante los próximos tres días _____

E. *Entrevista.* Practice interviewing someone, using the written cues. Give your questions when you hear the corresponding number. You will hear a possible question on the tape, as well as an answer to your question.

1. ¿dónde / ser?

6. ¿casado?

2. ¿dónde / vivir ahora?

7. ¿tener hijos?

3. ¿dónde / vivir antes?

8. ¿gustar hacer / si pudiera?

4. ¿dónde / trabajar?

9. ¿qué hacer / en el futuro?

5. ¿cuánto tiempo hace / trabajar allí?

F. *Entrevista.* You will hear a series of questions. Each will be said twice. Answer, based on your own experience. You will hear a possible answer on the tape.

1. ...   2. ...   3. ...   4. ...   5. ...

Capítulo 19

PRIMERA PARTE

VOCABULARIO: PREPARACIÓN

A. *Definiciones.* You will hear a series of definitions. Each will be said twice. Write the number of the definition next to the word or phrase that is best defined by each. First, listen to the list of words and phrases.

_____ viajar a otro país   _____ una multa

_____ la planilla de inmigración   _____ la frontera

_____ la nacionalidad   _____ el pasaporte

B. *¿Un hotel de lujo o una pensión pequeña?* You will hear a series of statements. Each will be said twice. Circle the letter of the place that is best described by each.

1. a) un hotel de lujo   b) una pensión pequeña

2. a) un hotel de lujo   b) una pensión pequeña

3. a) un hotel de lujo   b) una pensión pequeña

4. a) un hotel de lujo   b) una pensión pequeña

5. a) un hotel de lujo   b) una pensión pequeña

6. a) un hotel de lujo   b) una pensión pequeña

C. *Recuerdos de un viaje al extranjero.* You have recently returned from a trip abroad and your friends want to know all the details. Tell them some of the things that happened, using the oral cues. You will hear a possible answer on the tape.

1. ...   2. ...   3. ...   4. ...   5. ...

CH. *Descripción.* Describe what these people are doing, using the verbs you will hear. You will hear a possible answer on the tape.

1. ...   2. ...   3. ...   4. ...   5. ...

D. *Preguntas.* You will hear a series of questions. Each will be said twice. Answer, using words chosen from the following list. Make any necessary changes or additions to complete your answers. First, listen to the list.

propina	cheques de viajero
pensión	confirmar
huésped	recepción

1. ...   2. ...   3. ...   4. ...   5. ...   6. ...

E. *Conversación: En la recepción.* You will hear a conversation, partially printed in your manual, about getting a hotel room. Then you will participate in a similar conversation about another hotel. Complete it, based on the cues suggested. You will hear a possible answer on the tape.

—¿Cuál es la tarifa de una habitación _____?

—¿Con _____?

—Con _____ .

— _____ pesos la noche, señor.

—Está bien. Quisiéramos quedarnos _____ .

—Muy bien, señor. Me hace el favor de firmar aquí y de enseñarme su pasaporte.

Here are the cues for your conversation:

    media pensión
    almuerzo y cena, por favor
    cuatro noches

PRONUNCIACIÓN Y ORTOGRAFÍA: *NATIONALITIES*

A. Repeat the following names of countries and the nationalities of those who were born there.

1. Nicaragua - nicaragüense

    el Canadá - canadiense

    los Estados Unidos - estadounidense

    Costa Rica - costarricense

2. la Argentina - argentino/a

    el Perú - peruano/a

    Colombia - colombiano/a

    Bolivia - boliviano/a

3. el Uruguay - uruguayo/a

    el Paraguay - paraguayo/a

4. Honduras - hondureño/a

    Panamá - panameño/a

    el Brasil - brasileño/a

5. Guatemala - guatemalteco/a

    Portugal - portugués (portuguesa)

    Inglaterra - inglés (inglesa)

B. Now you will hear a series of nationalities. Each will be said twice. Repeat each and write the number of the nationality next to the country of origin. First, listen to the list of countries.

_____ Chile

_____ El Salvador

_____ Puerto Rico

_____ el Ecuador

_____ Venezuela

_____ Israel

MINIDIÁLOGOS Y GRAMÁTICA

52. *¿Por o para?* A Summary of Their Uses

A. *Minidiálogo: Antes de aterrizar.* You will hear a dialogue followed by a series of statements. Circle *C* if the statement is true or *F* if it is false.

1. C   F

2. C   F

3. C   F

4. C   F

B. *Reacciones*. You will hear a series of statements. Each will be said twice. Circle the letter of the most appropriate response to each.

1. a) ¿Por qué no lo llevamos a la sala de urgencias, por si acaso... ?
    b) ¡Por fin!

2. a) Pero por lo menos te mandó un regalo.
    b) ¿Por ejemplo?

3. a) ¿Por ejemplo?
    b) ¡Te digo que no, por última vez!

4. a) ¿Por qué tienes tanta sed?
    b) Ah, por eso tienes tanta sed.

5. a) Por el aumento que acaban de darme.
    b) Por dos horas.

C. *¿Qué hacen estas personas?* Using *por,* tell what the following people are doing when you hear the corresponding number. You will hear a possible answer on the tape.

MODELO:

→ Marcos habla por teléfono.

1.

2.

3.

4.

5.

CH. *¿Para qué están Uds. aquí?* Using the oral and written cues, tell why the people mentioned are in the locations you will hear on the tape. Each question will be said twice. First, listen to the list of reasons.

> ingresar dinero en la cuenta de ahorros
> hacer reservaciones para un viaje a Acapulco
> celebrar nuestro aniversario
> pedir un aumento de sueldo
> conseguir todos los detalles de la situación
> descansar y divertirse

> MODELO: los obreros (¿Para qué están los obreros en la dirección de personal?) →
> <u>Están allí para pedir un aumento de sueldo</u>.

1. Tina

2. el señor Guerra

3. mi esposo y yo

4. la familia Aragón

5. la reportera

D. *La vida diaria.* You will hear the following sentences followed by an oral cue. Extend each sentence, using *por* or *para*, as appropriate.

> MODELO: Hay que mandar los cheques. (miércoles) →
> Hay que mandar los cheques <u>para el miércoles</u>.

1. Salen el próximo mes.

2. Fueron al cine.

3. Estuvo en Honduras.

4. Habla muy bien el inglés.

5. A las ocho vamos a salir.

6. Venderían su coche viejo.

SEGUNDA PARTE

E. *Comentarios.* You will hear a series of descriptions or situations. Comment on each, using phrases chosen from the following list. Begin each answer with *Por eso...* Make any necessary changes or additions. First, listen to the list.

> estudiar / ser: mecánica / maestra
> caminar: parque / playa
> salir mañana: Aspen / Acapulco
>
> ir / mercado / comprar: vino / Coca-Cola
> correr: tarde / mañana

MODELO: (A Alida siempre le ha gustado jugar con todo tipo de máquina. Desde que era muy
            joven sabía arreglar relojes, tostadoras y otros aparatos pequeños.) →
            Por eso estudia para ser mecánica.

1. ...   2. ...   3. ...   4. ...

F. *En el periódico: Viajes.* The following ad appeared in a Mexican newspaper. You will hear a series of
statements about the ad. Circle *C* if the statement is true or *F* if it is false. First, scan the ad.

1. C F

2. C F

3. C F

4. C F

VACACIONES...?

Venga con su familia al Hotel Riviera del
Sol de Ixtapa y disfrute de un merecido
descanso en las soleadas playas y tibias
aguas del espléndido Pacífico Mexicano
y ahorre con nuestros tradicionales:

RIVIERA PAQUETES...!!!

/igencia: Julio 1° a Agosto 31, 1987

"RIVIERA PAQUETE DE PRIMAVERA"

3 NOCHES

4 DIAS

CON TRES DESAYUNOS

Precio por persona:
$ 80,000.00

Noche Extra:
$ 28,000.00

"PAQUETE MINI RIVIERA DE PRIMAVERA"

2 NOCHES

3 DIAS

CON DOS DESAYUNOS

Precio por persona:
$ 58,000.00

Noche Extra:
$ 28,000.00

SITUACIONES

A. *Viajando en el extranjero. Un viaje en el extranjero: En la aduana.* You will hear a conversation
between a traveler and a customs agent. Then you will hear a series of statements about the
conversation. Circle *C* if the statement is true or *F* if it is false.

1. C F   2. C F   3. C F   4. C F

B. *Conversación: Pasando por la aduana.* You will hear a conversation, partially printed in your manual,
between a customs inspector and a traveler. When it is read for the second time, take the role of the
traveler and complete the conversation, based on the cues suggested. You will hear a possible answer
on the tape.

INSPECTOR: ¿Cuál es su nacionalidad, por favor?

VIAJERO/A: _____.

INSPECTOR: ¿Me da su pasaporte, por favor?

VIAJERO/A: Sí, cómo no. Aquí _____.

INSPECTOR: ¿Tiene algo que declarar?

VIAJERO/A: Sí, compré _____ y _____, pero son para uso personal.

INSPECTOR: Abra su maleta, por favor.

VIAJERO/A: Un momento, por favor. Se la _____.

INSPECTOR: ¡Ud. tendrá que pagar una multa! Es ilegal llevar estas _____.

VIAJERO/A: Lo siento... de veras no sabía que era ilegal traer _____.

¿Cuánto es la multa?

INSPECTOR: Cuatrocientos pesos, por favor.

Here are the cues for your conversation:

canadiense / Toronto
blusa bordada a mano / par de zapatos
verduras

UN POCO DE TODO

A. *Diálogo: Problemas del viaje.* You will hear a brief dialogue between two friends, Ricardo and Luis, who are traveling abroad together. Then you will hear a series of statements about the dialogue. Circle *C* if the statement is true or *F* if it is false.

1. C F   2. C F   3. C F   4. C F

B. *Listening Passsage.* You will hear a brief passage about what you might see on a visit to Mexico. It will be read twice. Then you will hear a series of statements about the passage. Circle *C* if the statement is true or *F* if it is false. Answers to this exercise are given at the end of the tape.

1. C F   2. C F   3. C F   4. C F

C. *Conversación: Hablando de las raíces* (roots). You will hear a brief conversation. It will be read twice. Then you will hear the following incomplete sentences. Complete them, based on the conversation.

1. Mi familia emigró _____ la situación política de mi país era intolerable.

2. Ah, emigraron _____ necesidad.

3. _____ ser extranjera, hablas muy bien el inglés.

4. Tuve que aprender a hablar el inglés para sobrevivir en este país; _____ lo hablo tan bien.

CH. *Descripción*. Circle the letter of the picture best described by the sentences you hear. Each will be said twice.

1. a)  b)

2. a) 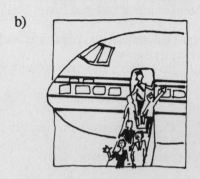 b)

3. a)  b)

4. a)  b)

D. *Entrevista*. You will hear a series of questions. Each will be said twice. Answer, based on your own experience. You will hear a possible answer on the tape.

1. ...   2. ...   3. ...   4. ...   5. ...   6. ...   7. ...

E. *Y para terminar… Una canción.* The song *La llorona* is a song of lost love.

La llorona

Todos me dicen el negro, llorona,		
Negro, pero cariñoso;	(*bis*)	
Yo soy como el chile verde, llorona,		
Picante,* pero sabroso.*	(*bis*)	*Spicy / tasty*
Ay de mi llorona,		
Llorona de ayer y hoy;	(*bis*)	
Ayer maravilla* fui, llorona,		*marvel*
Y ahora ni sombra* soy.	(*bis*)	*ni… not even a shadow*
Dicen que no tengo duelo,* llorona,		*sorrow*
Porque no me ven llorar;	(*bis*)	
Hay muertos que no hacen ruido, llorona,		
Y es más grande su penar.*	(*bis*)	*pain*

Capítulo 20

VOCABULARIO: PREPARACIÓN

A. *¿Dónde están?* You will hear a series of brief conversations or parts of conversations. Write the number of the conversation next to the location where it might have taken place. You will hear a possible answer on the tape. First, listen to the list of locations.

_____ una pastelería   _____ una farmacia

_____ un estanco   _____ la estación del metro

_____ una papelería   _____ un café

B. *Descripción.* Identify the following items when you hear the corresponding number. Begin each sentence with *Es...* or *Son...*

1. ...   2. ...   3. ...   4. ...   5. ...   6. ...   7. ...   8. ...

C. *Conversación: En Madrid.* You will hear a conversation, partially printed in your manual, about going shopping. Then you will participate in two similar conversations. Complete them, based on the cues suggested and the name of the store or place where one could buy the products named. You will hear a possible answer on the tape.

—Necesito _____ . ¿Quieres acompañarme?

—Cómo no. ¿Adónde vas?

—Hay _____ cerca, ¿no?

— _____ .

Here is the cue for your first conversation:

        mandarles un paquete a mis padres

Here is the cue for your second conversation:

        el último número de *El País*

PRONUNCIACIÓN Y ORTOGRAFÍA: *REPASO GENERAL*

A. When you hear the corresponding number, read the following Hispanic proverbs, then listen to the correct pronunciation and repeat it.

1. Llamar al pan, pan y al vino, vino.

2. El agua para bañarse, el vino para beberse.

3. Quien mucho duerme, poco aprende.

4. No hay mal que por bien (*for a good reason*) no venga.

5. No hay regla sin excepción.

6. No hay montaña tan alta que un asno (*burro*) cargado de oro no la suba.

B. Listen to the following paragraph, then read it in the pause provided. You may want to record your reading.

Madrid, 7 de marzo

Querido Joe,

¡Cuánto me alegro de que por fin te hayas animado a escribirme y más todavía por eso que me cuentas de que tal vez te decidas a pasar un año en España! ¡Me parece genial! Has mejorado mucho tu español en estos últimos meses y, desde luego, un año en mi país sería perfecto.

C. *Dictado.* You will hear six sentences. Each will be said twice. Write what you hear.

1. _____

2. _____

3. _____

4. _____

5. _____

6. _____

UN POCO DE TODO

A. *En el periódico: Anuncios.* The following ads appeared in a Spanish newspaper. Look at them and choose one place in which you would like to study Spanish. Scan that ad. Then answer the questions you hear, based on the ad you chose. If the information requested is not given in the ad, say *No lo dice.* No answers will be given on the tape.

UNIVERSIDAD DE CANTABRIA

CURSO INTENSIVO DE VERANO

LAREDO, SANTANDER / JULY 13-AUGUST 7

⇨ Intensive "Survival Spanish".   ⇨ Housing available.
⇨ Cultural activities.   ⇨ Certificate of Aptitude from
⇨ Sports facilities.   University of Cantabria.

Fundación Ponce de León
Lagasca, 16 - 28001 Madrid
Tel. (91) 435 65 00

CURSOS DE ESPAÑOL EN VALENCIA (ESPAÑA)

CURSOS DURANTE TODO EL AÑO

4 horas diarias y alojamiento
con familias españolas

Información: C. I. L. C. E.
Bordadores, 10, 46001 Valencia
Teléfono 331 04 63

1. ...   2. ...   3. ...   4. ...   5. ...   6. ...

B. *De vacaciones en el extranjero.* You will hear a brief paragraph describing a series of actions and events. It will be read twice. Number the actions listed below from one to ten in the order in which they occur in the paragraph.

First, listen to the list of actions.

_____ aterrizar en Madrid

_____ hacer las maletas

_____ recoger los boletos

_____ despegar otra vez

__9__ pasar por la aduana

__1__ visitar la agencia de viajes

_____ ir al hotel

_____ sentarse en la sección de fumar

_____ bajar del avión

__5__ hacer una escala en Londres (*London*)

C. *Listening Passsage.* You will hear a brief passage about studying abroad. It will be read twice. Then you will hear a series of incomplete statements about the passage. Circle the letter of the phrase that best completes each statement. Answers to this exercise are given at the end of the tape.

1. a)   ...pasará todo el tiempo en clase
    b)   ...tendrá tiempo de explorar la ciudad donde vive

2. a)   ...debe informarse del clima de la región
    b)   ...debe lavar su ropa

3. a)   ...es mejor no llevar aparatos eléctricos
    b)   ...debería llevar muchos aparatos eléctricos

4. a)   ...será planeado por el estudiante
    b)   ...ya ha sido planeado para el estudiante

5. a)   ...sólo encontrará estudiantes americanos
    b)   ...conocerá a estudiantes hispanos y extranjeros

CH. *Descripción: ¿Unos discos estupendos?* You will hear a series of questions. Each will be said twice. Answer, based on the following cartoon. You will hear a possible answer on the tape. As you look at the cartoon and listen to the questions, keep in mind that the tourist in the drawing wants to go to Kiland, an imaginary country where Kiland is spoken.

1. ...   2. ...   3. ...   4. ...   5. ...   6. ...

D. *Entrevista final.* You will hear a series of questions or situations followed by questions. Each will be said twice. Answer, based on your own experience. Model answers will be given on the tape for the last two questions.

1. ...   2. ...   3. ...   4. ...   5. ...   6. ...

E. *Y para terminar... Una canción. Triste y sola* is a traditional song sung by Spanish university students.

Triste y sola

Triste y sola,
Sola se queda Fonseca.
Triste y llorosa*   *tearful*
Queda la Universidad.
Y los libros,
Y los libros empeñados*   *pawned, in hock*
En el monte,*   montaña
En el monte de piedad.*   *pity*

No te acuerdas cuando te decía
A la pálida luz de la luna:
«Yo no puedo querer más que a una,
Y esa una, mi vida, eres tú.»

Triste y sola... (*bis*)

Answers *to* Dictados

ANTE TODO 1

p. 4 1. Héctor 2. Enrique 3. Yolanda 4. Begoña 5. Concha 6. Juana **p. 5** 1. Nicolás es pesimista. 2. La profesora Díaz es inteligente. 3. Don Juan no es sincero. 4. Maite es muy eficiente. 5. Íñigo no es sentimental.

ANTE TODO 2

p. 6 1. Naciones: Italia 2. Instrumentos musicales: piano, clarinete 3. Personas: dentista, turista 4. Animales: tigre 5. Cosas: radio, bomba **p. 7** 1. paso 2. casa 3. mesa 4. cine 5. pesar 6. misa **p. 7** veintiocho dos seis cero doce trece veinticuatro tres

ANTE TODO 3

p. 10 1. ¿Dónde está? 2. ¿Quién es el estudiante? 3. ¿Qué es esto? 4. ¿Cuánto es el chocolate? 5. ¿A qué hora es la excursión? 6. ¿Cuál es la capital?

CAPÍTULO 1

p. 17 1. Alicia es amable. 2. Pili estudia español. 3. ¿Cómo está usted? 4. Hay veintisiete estudiantes en clase hoy. **p. 18** 1. una residencia 2. un dependiente 3. una mujer 4. una mochila 5. un hotel 6. un secretario 7. un bolígrafo 8. una mesa 9. una universidad **p. 19** Singular: el escritorio, un bolígrafo, un cuaderno Plural: unos lápices, unos papeles, las sillas, unos libros **p. 22** ella: habla nosotras: practicamos, deseamos yo: trabajo, tomo

CAPÍTULO 2

p. 29 45 mochilas 99 lápices 52 cuadernos 75 novelas 31 calculadoras 100 libros de texto **p. 31** 1. papá 2. música 3. práctico 4. nación 5. doctor 6. Marina 7. joven 8. inteligente 9. biología

CAPÍTULO 3

p. 46 la lámpara: 2.615 pesetas el televisor: 14.442 pesetas el escritorio con silla: 12.150 pesetas la calculadora: 1.320 pesetas el vestido: 9.989 pesetas un par de zapatos: 3.740 pesetas

REPASO 1

p. 47 el nombre del almacén: Carrillo el precio de los zapatos para señora: 20 dólares el precio de los trajes para caballero: cien dólares tres cosas para el hogar: estéreos, radios, refrigeradores, sillas, sofás, computadoras el precio del estéreo: 900 dólares el precio del sofá: 300 dólares

CAPÍTULO 4

p. 51   Check the script against what you wrote in the chart: <u>El martes y el jueves</u> tengo una clase de literatura española a las tres de la tarde.   <u>El miércoles</u> a la una tengo que ir a la biblioteca.   <u>El miércoles</u> también debo hablar con la profesora Díaz a las nueve de la mañana.   <u>El lunes y el viernes</u>, enseño una clase de conversación a las once menos cuarto de la mañana.   <u>El viernes</u> a las nueve y media de la noche hay una fiesta para los estudiantes extranjeros.   <u>El martes</u> a las diez y quince de la mañana tengo que comprar bolígrafos y papel en la librería.   También tengo que ir al dentista <u>el martes</u> , creo que a las ocho y treinta de la mañana.   **p. 53**   1. Tomás también bebe cerveza.   2. ¿Van a venir el viernes o el sábado?   3. La abuela de Belinda es baja.   4. Vas al baile el jueves, ¿verdad?   **p. 57**   1. Esta señora es la madre del novio y aquel señor es el padre.   2. Estos regalos son para los novios.   3. Esa señorita es la hermana de la novia y aquella mujer es su prima.   4. ¿Y qué es esto? Es el champán para la recepción.   **p. 58**   El día de la semana en que tuvo lugar la boda: <u>el viernes</u>   La hora de la boda: <u>a las seis de la tarde</u>   Los nombres de los esposos: <u>Hortensia y Roberto</u>   ¿Hubo recepción después de la boda? <u>sí</u>

CAPÍTULO 5

p. 66   1. Esta película es <u>mejor</u> que aquélla. Por eso hay <u>más de</u> cien personas en este cine.   2. Nati tiene <u>tantos</u> hermanos como hermanas. Su hermanito Ángel tiene <u>menos de</u> diez años. Es el <u>menor</u>.   3. En el desierto hace <u>más</u> calor durante el día que durante la noche. Durante el día, la temperatura llega a <u>más de</u> treinta grados centígrados.

CAPÍTULO 6

p. 73   1. cuatro   2. quince   3. cálculo   4. compras   5. parque   6. rico   **p. 79**   el nombre del restaurante: <u>«La Paloma»</u>   la dirección: <u>la Calle la Reforma, número 1500</u>   la especialidad de la casa: <u>los mariscos</u>   otros platos que se sirven allí: <u>chuletas de cerdo, pollo frito, jamón y bistec</u>   el horario: <u>seis días a la semana de las once y media de la mañana hasta las doce de la noche; los domingos, de las seis de la tarde hasta las diez de la noche</u>   ¿Se recomienda hacer reservaciones? <u>sí</u>

CAPÍTULO 7

p. 87   1. Paco toca el piano para sus parientes.   2. Los tíos de Tito son de Puerto Rico.   3. ¿Por qué gastas tanto en ropa?   4. Tito trabaja para el padre de Pepe, ¿verdad?   **p. 90**   1. deciden   2. cenar   3. es   4. Julio   5. mexicano   6. porque   7. esposo   8. él   9. gusta   10. llegan   11. les   12. reservada   13. les   14. demasiado   15. orquesta   16. está   17. mejor   18. le   19. al   20. leerlo   21. le   22. quieren   23. les   24. Después   25. le   26. pastel   27. al   28. los   29. cuenta   30. pagar   31. gustaría   32. cumpleaños

CAPÍTULO 8

p. 102   el nombre de la empresa: <u>Redana, S.A.</u>   el nombre del entrevistador: <u>el Sr. Delgado</u>   el nombre de la aspirante: <u>la Srta. Prados</u>   lo que estudia la aspirante: <u>comercio internacional</u>   la fecha de graduación de la aspirante: <u>el 15 de mayo de este año</u>

CAPÍTULO 9

p. 108   1. Don Guillermo es viejo y generoso.   2. Por lo general, los jóvenes de hoy son inteligentes.   3. El consejero de los estudiantes extranjeros es de Gijón.   4. Juana estudia geografía y geología.   5. Mi amiga Gloria y yo gastamos mucho dinero.

REPASO 3

p. 117   el tipo de boleto que el turista quiere: <u>un boleto de ida y vuelta</u>   la fecha de salida: <u>el doce de noviembre</u>   la fecha de regreso: <u>el veintisiete de noviembre</u>   la sección y la clase en que va a viajar: <u>la sección de no fumar, en primera clase</u>   la ciudad de la cual va a salir el avión: <u>Chicago</u>   el tipo de hotel que quiere: <u>uno que esté frente a la playa y que tenga aire acondicionado</u>   el nombre del hotel en que se va a quedar: <u>el Hotel Presidente</u>

CAPÍTULO 10

p. 121   1. El cumpleaños de Begoña es mañana.   2. La señorita Marañón estudia mucho.   3. Los señores Ibáñez son los dueños del Hotel España.   4. Esa muchacha es chilena.

CAPÍTULO 11

p. 131   1. A ellos <u>se les olvidó</u> el número de teléfono de Marta.   2. A Juan <u>se le perdieron</u> los anteojos. 3. No quiero que <u>se nos quede</u> el equipaje en el aeropuerto.   4. A los niños <u>se les rompieron</u> los juguetes.

CAPÍTULO 12

p. 135   Estuve <u>muy enfermo</u> la semana pasada. El lunes, cuando me desperté, <u>tenía fiebre</u> y <u>me dolía</u> la cabeza. También estaba un poco <u>mareado</u> y no podía <u>respirar</u> bien. El martes <u>empecé</u> a <u>toser</u>, pero <u>lo peor</u> fue que me dolía <u>todo</u> el <u>cuerpo</u>. Por fin <u>hice</u> una cita con el <u>médico</u> para el miércoles y él <u>me recetó</u> un <u>antibiótico</u>. Desafortunadamente <u>tuve</u> que <u>guardar cama</u> por tres días y <u>falté</u> al trabajo el resto de la <u>semana</u>. Como no tenía apetito, no <u>comí bien</u> y perdí tres o cuatro libras. <u>Esta</u> semana, gracias a Dios, <u>me siento mejor</u>. ¡Espero que no me vuelva a <u>enfermar</u> este año!

CAPÍTULO 13

p. 151   1. Todos estaban enfermos ayer.   2. A Ana le dolían los ojos y a Irma le dolía el pie izquierdo. 3. Juan acaba de ir a la sala de urgencia.   4. Carlos estaba mareado y se acostó temprano.

CAPÍTULO 14

p. 158   1. ¿Cuál es tu profesión? ¿Te pagan bien?   2. Tú no la conoces, ¿verdad?   3. ¿Prefiere Ud. que le sirva la comida en el patio?   4. ¡Qué ejercicio más fácil!   5. No sé dónde viven, pero sí sé su número de teléfono.

CAPÍTULO 15

p. 166   1. jugó   2. jugo   3. describes   4. descríbemela   5. sicología   6. sicólogo   7. almacén 8. almacenes   9. levántate   10. levanta   11. gusto   12. gustó   **p. 172**   cuándo tiene lugar la función: <u>el viernes, doce de abril a las nueve de la noche</u>.   el nombre de la comedia: <u>«Sol de invierno»</u> la actriz principal: <u>Corazón Aguilar</u>   el nombre del teatro: <u>el Teatro Nacional</u>   el nombre de las personas que van a la función: <u>Marta, Mercedes y Roberto</u>

REPASO 5

p. 175   el nombre de los equipos que van a jugar: <u>los Jefes y las Panteras</u>   el nombre de las personas que van al partido: <u>Teresa y Ricardo</u>   lo que no le gusta a Héctor: <u>los deportes</u>   la hora que empieza el partido: <u>a las siete de la noche</u>   lo que van a hacer Héctor y su amiga: <u>ver una película (comedia)</u>

CAPÍTULO 16

p. 179   1. los demás   2. la dictadura   3. la esperanza   4. durar   **p. 180**   1. Creo <u>que ese</u> regalo es para <u>mí</u>.   2. Aquí <u>está tu té</u>. ¿Qué más quieres?   3. <u>Él</u> dijo <u>que te</u> iba a llamar a las ocho.   4. <u>Sí, mi</u> amigo <u>se</u> llama Antonio.   **p. 184**   el nombre de la candidata que perdió las elecciones: <u>Quejada</u>   el nombre del candidato que ganó las elecciones: <u>Muñoz</u>   el porcentaje de los ciudadanos que votó por la candidata que perdió: <u>treinta por ciento</u>   la cuestión principal de la campaña: <u>la pena de muerte</u>   **p. 184**   1. fuimos 2. resultó   3. Íbamos   4. pasar   5. saliéramos   6. dimos   7. teníamos   8. cambiamos   9. pusimos 10. notamos   11. había   12. olvidado   13. perdimos   14. Pasamos   15. manejando   16. quería 17. regresáramos   18. insistió   19. siguiéramos   20. buscando   21. encontramos   22. empezó 23. dejó   24. llover   25. volvimos   26. quisiera   27. quedarme

CAPÍTULO 17

p. 187   1. quejarse   2. el alquiler   3. gastar   4. el sueldo   **p. 189**   1. fosfato   2. atención 3. amoníaco   4. teología   5. oposición   6. fotografía   7. colección   8. arquitecto
p. 190   PRETÉRITO: presté, se enojó, devolví   FUTURO: aprenderá, Pagaremos, podré
p. 191   1. cobre   2. puedan   3. visitan   4. dejó

CAPÍTULO 18

p. 198   Las quejas de los empleados: 1. Siempre dicen que somos perezosos.   2. Nunca nos dan los aumentos que pedimos.   3. Creo que ellos ganan mucho más que nosotros.   Las quejas de los jefes: 4. Nunca llegan a tiempo.   5. Siempre quieren que les demos un aumento.   6. Nunca quieren quedarse a trabajar después de las cinco.

REPASO 6

p. 207   la fecha del noticiero: <u>el lunes, ocho de enero de 1989</u>   el tiempo que hace: <u>ha nevado mucho</u> el nombre de la fábrica donde terminó la huelga: <u>Barrera</u>   lo qué decidió darles a los obreros el dueño de la fábrica: <u>un pequeño aumento de sueldo</u>   la fecha en que regresan al trabajo los obreros: <u>el quince de enero</u> el mes en que se jugará el campeonato: <u>febrero</u>   la temperatura alta durante los próximos tres días: <u>20 grados Fahrenheit</u>

CAPÍTULO 20

p. 220   1. Cuando viajes a Madrid, no olvides tu cámara.   2. ¿Quisieras tomar una copita conmigo en el bar?   3. Había mucha gente en la parada del autobús.   4. Mandaría la carta si tuviera sellos y un sobre. 5. Perdón, señora, ¿dónde está la estación del metro?   6. No creo que le haya gustado el batido que le sirvieron.